THE HOLY LAND AS JESUS KNEW IT

Its People, Customs, and Religion

David K. O'Rourke, O.P.

LIGUORI
PUBLICATIONS

One Liguori Drive
Liguori, Missouri 63057
(314) 464-2500

Imprimi Potest:
John F. Dowd, C.SS.R.
Provincial, St. Louis Province
Redemptorist Fathers

Imprimatur:
Monsignor Edward J. O'Donnell
Vicar General, Archdiocese of St. Louis

ISBN 0-89243-182-2
Library of Congress Catalog Card Number: 83-80856

Copyright © 1983, Liguori Publications
Printed in U.S.A.

Cover design — Pam Hummelsheim
Cover photograph — Lew Gordon
All interior illustrations by — P. Kaler

All interior photographs are the property of the author, with the
following exceptions:
    R. Boever — 41 top, 59, 65, 76, 84, 98 top, 118, 141
    G. Clark — 150
    P. Kaler — 12, 87, 93 bottom, 98 bottom, 132
    N. Muckerman — 15, 41 bottom, 56, 85

ACKNOWLEDGEMENTS

Any text involving biblical topics is obviously indebted to the historians, exegetes, linguists, and archaeologists whose scholarly work forms the body of knowledge that is being treated. In the fall of 1955, as a young man just out of college and having recently experienced a conversion, I arrived in the small Provençal town of St. Maximin-La Ste. Baume. I had gone there to study in a seven-hundred-years-old Dominican monastery that was a center of theological and biblical studies. Under the direction of Père Ephrem Lauzière, O.P., I was introduced to the Scriptures, to scriptural scholarship, and to the lessons to be learned from the stones of ancient civilizations. In recognizing this first teacher, I wish to acknowledge, symbolically, the many others who have taught me in the intervening twenty-five years.

In addition, I want to thank all my friends and colleagues who helped in the preparation of this manuscript. I want, especially, to acknowledge a bequest from the estate of Grace Camp which helped substantially in the on-site work that went into the writing.

I wish to thank my brother John, who graciously surrendered the study in his country house to maps, photos, papers, and shards during the months it took me to complete the manuscript. I also wish to thank Barbara Finley and Leo Thomas, O.P., who read the manuscript and who made very useful comments for its reediting. Finally, I wish to thank Patrick Kaler, C.SS.R., of Liguori Publications for his ongoing assistance as the manuscript was prepared for publication.

TABLE OF CONTENTS

The Holy Land in the days of Christ

INTRODUCTION

"They then took charge of Jesus, and carrying his own cross he went out of the city to the place of the skull or, as it was called in Hebrew, Golgotha, where they crucified him . . . the place where Jesus was crucified was not far from the city . . . At the place where he had been crucified there was a garden, and in this garden a new tomb in which no one had yet been buried. Since it was the Jewish Day of Preparation and the tomb was near at hand, they laid Jesus there" (John 19:17-18,20,41-42).

About twenty years before the birth of Christ, King Herod the Great began one of his most ambitious projects. This renowned builder, who left the world one of its greatest collections of monuments, decided to undertake a building project as daring as it was difficult. He planned to rebuild Jerusalem, literally, from the ground up. He would replace the narrow and winding streets with wide avenues laid out at regular intervals. He would strengthen its walls, embellish its public buildings, enlarge and rebuild its aqueducts, and renew its fortifications. As the crowning glory of his reign he would tear down the great Temple in Jerusalem, the very center of the Jewish world, and rebuild it to be even more splendid than the Temple built by King Solomon himself. He would make Jerusalem a marvel, a political and religious capital known and respected throughout the world.

King Herod the Great achieved what he set out to do. Every one of these goals was achieved during his life or by his immediate successors. And the Romans, who looked in wonder at this bizarre, cruel, and complex Near Eastern prince, were still quite happy to count him as their ally.

Herod set an army of men to work on his project. Their rebuilding required a mountain of stone. In our age of machines and power tools we have a hard time imagining a world powered only by muscle. Yet that is what rebuilt Jerusalem — the muscles of men and animals — arms, backs, legs, and shoulders applied to rope, lever, and yoke. To keep this effort to a reasonable limit Herod's quarrymen used sources that were as close to the con-

7

struction site as possible. Today we have machines to bring the building materials to the work site. Herod's men had to carry and pull their stone blocks from the quarries to the building sites, so they chose their quarries carefully.

The Most Sacred Place

One quarry they created just outside the walls of Jerusalem is the focal point of our interest. It has become the most sacred place in the Christian world. It is of special interest to us at the beginning of this history not only because it is the holiest place in the Holy Land but also because it sums up the difficulties we face in trying to reconstruct history.

Looking back two thousand years is a formidable task. Looking back through two thousand years marked by wars, destruction, burnings, and conquest is especially difficult. The historical record, quite literally, is in torn fragments, in broken pieces, and in ruins. Fortunately for us there are scholars today, scientists of the past, who are refitting and studying the fragments, reassembling the broken pieces, and analyzing and even reconstructing the ruins. The history of this quarry, the way it was excavated, used, changed, and rediscovered, gives us a prime example of the help we receive from scholars. We will look at this quarry at the beginning of our history as an example of the use we will make of the work of historians, archaeologists, and biblical scholars in our study of the Holy Land in the time of Christ.

When the stonecutters began to look for the materials needed for the city's rebuilding they did not have to look very far. Jerusalem is built on rock, and it is surrounded by other rock hills. All they needed to do was step outside the city walls and look under their feet. That is what they did.

On the northwest side of Jerusalem a wall once ran from the upper city eastward to the Antonia fortress. Right outside that wall's location the quarrymen began their work. As they cut into the stone, layer by layer, they discovered that part of it was flawed. There was a cracked and inferior section of stone that ran from the surface down into the rock. Needless to say, that flawed section was unusable for building blocks. So the workers did what any reasonable man would do. They cut around it. It would be a terrible waste of energy to remove the flawed section, and it would be a pointless waste of a good quarry site to abandon the whole place because of the flaw. When they had finished with their quarrying they had partly cleared out a new space outside the walls. For reasons we shall soon see, its dimensions are unknown to us. But somewhere within it stood that section of flawed stone, an outcropping rising about thirty feet from the floor of the quarry to where the top of the hill had been. At the perimeter were the flat, stone surfaces of the quarry walls. It was not long before these man-made bluffs were put to a use quite common in the Jerusalem area. Holes were cut into the walls, chambers large enough to entomb the bodies of the dead.

The "Hill" of Calvary

Shortly after the days of King Herod this quarry was put to another, more grisly use. Because it was just outside the walls and so near one of the city's main gates, many people passed by at every hour of the day. The flawed stone, now surrounded by the debris and refuse of several dozen years, formed a little hill, high enough to be seen by passersby. Here criminals were put to death. An upright beam was fixed in the flawed stone. The poor unfortunates sentenced to crucifixion, and there were hundreds of them, would be brought here and to similar places, dragging a shorter beam along with them. Their arms would be tied to the short beam, it would be hoisted to the top of the fixed upright, and they would be left there. For several days they would hang there, finally and mercifully dying, an object lesson to anyone who dared challenge authority.

The Tomb of Jesus

In the Gospel of Saint John we read that at the place where Jesus was crucified there was a garden, and in the garden a new tomb, and this was near at hand. Christian tradition identifies this quarry with the site of the execution, burial, and Resurrection of Jesus. On this site stands the Church of the Holy Sepulcher. Yet, the pilgrim going to this church will look in vain for anything even vaguely resembling a quarry, a small hill, a garden, or a tomb. Why is this? To answer this question and to trace the connection between the quarry and today's church we need the assistance of the historians, archaeologists, and biblical scholars. We will look briefly at what they have to say.

What do we have to start with? First there is the tradition of the Christian community in Jerusalem which prayed at the tomb of Jesus. It was, and still is, a custom in the Holy Land to honor and pray at the graves of holy men. The early Christians prayed at Christ's tomb, the early tradition tells us, until the Jewish revolt of A.D. 66 brought about their dispersal.

We know that in A.D. 135 the Emperor Hadrian built a temple to Aphrodite near the site, filling in the quarry to do so. The temple stood there until A.D. 326, when the Emperor Constantine, a convert to Christianity, built his monumental church. Historians tell us that Constantine's choice of the site is significant. In Rome Constantine built several major and monumental basilicas. He did so on his own private land, outside the city, so as not to offend the non-Christian aristocracy and their priesthood. His power in Rome was not so well established that he could afford to step on their toes. That he was willing to remove a pagan temple in Jerusalem and to undertake the expense and trouble of removing other substantial buildings, when a move to a site a few hundred feet away would have been so much simpler, is an indication that this location, and no other, was the place to be honored.

Constantine's Building

Archaeologists have been able to reconstruct the floor plans of Constantine's building, which was actually a complex of buildings. Going from front to back it included a stairway leading up to a large atrium; a rectangular basilica for public worship entered from the atrium; an open courtyard directly in back of the basilica; an extensive colonnaded shrine encircling the tomb on the far side of the courtyard. From front to back the building measured almost five hundred feet. The construction around the tomb itself comprised a small stone shrine enclosing the tomb proper, then a very impressive circle of large, high columns surrounding the shrine and supporting a dome. The dome was added well after Constantine's death.

The church remained much the same until the year A.D. 1009. The Moslems had captured Jerusalem in A.D. 638, but had permitted Christian pilgrims to continue their voyages to the holy places. However, in 1009 the mad Caliph Hakim destroyed the church. His workers took sledges to the tomb of Christ. A generation later Hakim's son permitted the Christians to rebuild the church as best they could, but their efforts were limited to the area around the shrine. It was around A.D. 1150 that the Crusaders arrived. They built the church that we see today.

The Church of the Holy Sepulcher

If we look at the Crusaders' church and try to envisage the quarry of Herod's time or the hillock called Golgotha or Calvary or the church that Constantine built, we will not succeed. Pilgrims entering the present church find that it raises as many questions as it may answer. It is an unusual building. It is not entered through an imposing doorway off a dignified plaza, like St. Peter's in Rome or the shrine at Lourdes, but through a side door leading off a small square.

Inside there are three main sections, plus many little chapels. There is a large, walled-in section in the center of the church. By its location it would seem to be the most important part of the church. In fact, it is the area used for public worship by the Greek Orthodox, and points out that this is primarily a Greek Orthodox church. This walled-in chapel is artistically beautiful and religiously impressive but of lesser interest to the pilgrims than the other two sections.

Facing the entrance to the Orthodox sanctuary is the small, marble shrine less than two hundred years old, but prevented from collapse only by steel supports. This little house is in the center of the circle of columns supporting the main dome of the church, and so is directly under the dome. The building is on the site of Jesus' tomb. Some maintain that part of the stone of his tomb can still be seen inside the building. Others maintain that whatever Hakim's destroyers left intact was destroyed by the stone-cracking fire that charred the interior of the church in the early nineteenth century.

Just inside the door of the church there is a long, steep flight of stairs that goes up to a second-floor balcony. At the rear of this balcony there is a low-ceilinged chapel. This balcony and chapel are at the level of the top of the hillock of flawed stone, and it is the site of the crucifixion, the chapel of Calvary.

The second floor Greek Orthodox Calvary chapel in the Church of the Holy Sepulcher. The top of the rock itself can be touched by extending the hand through a hole (see arrow) in the paving under the altar.

How do we connect what we know of the crucifixion and burial of Christ with the Church of the Holy Sepulcher? If the tomb was cut into the wall of a quarry, how could it have been surrounded by columns and covered with a dome? If the crucifixion took place on the top of the hillock of flawed stone, how could it now be in the upstairs chapel of an eleventh century church? And if this is really the holiest site in Christendom, why does it look so jumbled and unimpressive?

There are four key words that will give us the answers we need to connect the quarry of Herod's workers with the church we see today. These are the words that unlock the knowledge of the archaeologists, historians, and biblical scholars. The words are resurrection, pilgrimage, worship, and scandal. We will draw on the work of the scholars to explain these words.

Resurrection

Historians tell us that for the first Christians, beginning with the followers of Christ in Jerusalem during the first thirty years after his death, nothing was as important to them as the fact that he had been raised from the dead. That their Friend and Master, who had been put to death so cruelly, was now raised from the dead was the central fact of their faith and their life.

As sign and symbol of that Resurrection they had his empty tomb. No place was as important to them as this spot. In the Holy Land, as we noted above, it was and is the custom to venerate the tombs of holy men, and it quickly became the practice to gather at this tomb both to do honor to God and to recall the fact of Jesus' Resurrection from the dead.

The place of the crucifixion was an honored spot, as were all the places central to his life. But the horror of crucifixion was still too present a reality, the places of crucifixion and the bodies of the crucified still too much a part of Roman rule to be faced with anything but dread. Further, there is no reason to assume that the hillock used for Jesus' execution was not still being used to crucify other unfortunates. His tomb, on the other hand, belonged to his followers the way any tomb was considered the property of surviving family and friends.

The Christian Church of the first centuries was a Church of the risen Christ. The suffering and death of Jesus did not become so centrally important in the piety of the people until the beginning of the Middle Ages. When Constantine decided to honor the most important site in the life of Jesus what was honored was his tomb, the empty tomb, the symbol of the risen Christ. Constantine's church was not called the Church of the Holy Sepulcher. That was the name the Crusaders gave to their church. His church was called the Church of the Resurrection.

This Church of the Resurrection that Constantine began in the year A.D. 326 was to be a place of pilgrimage. To understand why it was built with the rectangular basilica and the circular, domed area separated by a courtyard we have to look to our scholars again. This time we look to them for an explanation of our second key word, pilgrimage.

Pilgrimage

Were we to make a pilgrimage today we might think of going to a holy place, like the tomb of Saint Peter in Rome or one of the shrines in the Holy Land, and praying there privately or spending some time in our meditations, attending a liturgy, etc. For the pilgrim in the Middle East a pilgrimage meant something different. It meant going to the holy place and walking around it. Literally, walking around it. And for some peoples it meant walking around it three times. This circling was not just a Christian custom. It was a Middle Eastern custom, honored even today. When Moslem pilgrims go to Mecca today their pilgrimage reaches its high point when, after washing, they walk around the Kaa'ba, the small building containing the black stone which, according to Moslem belief, was given by the angel Gabriel to Abraham.

When Constantine came to build his church in honor of the Resurrection he wanted to build a monumental focal point for the Christian pilgrim. But he faced a problem. The tomb of Jesus was carved in the wall of a quarry. How can you walk around a quarry at all, let alone in any religious and dignified way? The answer was as simple as its implementation was difficult. He would have to cut away that part of the wall and the hillside surrounding the tomb of Christ until the area of rock containing the tomb would stand alone. Historians tell us that the church, begun in the year 326, was dedicated in 335. However, isolating the tomb from the quarry took a few more years, an indication of the difficulty and the scope of the effort. The workers removed about five thousand cubic yards of stone in the form of building blocks, and a circular area over a hundred feet wide was created.

Now the pilgrims coming to Jerusalem would be able to walk within the colonnade around the tomb of Jesus. In the same way

One of the ancient tombs in the Kidron Valley. It illustrates how such tombs and mausoleums were carved from the solid rock cliff.

St. Peter's house at Capernaum. The octagonal church is a fifth-century construction on top of a fourth-century church, which, in turn, was built around a central room venerated since the middle of the first century.

they could walk around his house in Capernaum, for that house had also had an octagonal, covered walkway added around it for pilgrims. Similarly, a few hundred years later, Moslem pilgrims would begin walking the octagonal pavement around the sacred stone within the Dome of the Rock, the beautiful shrine on Jerusalem's Temple Mount.

Worship

With this means of completing a pilgrimage assured for the pilgrims to Christ's tomb, why would Constantine also build a monumental basilica just a few hundred feet away? To answer this question we will look at the third of our key words, worship. In the time of Constantine, much as it has been throughout the Christian world ever since, there was a difference between private devotion and public worship. Scholars tell us that proper worship required not only the shrine for private devotion but a building designed for public worship as well. This is what we find in the Church of the Resurrection. There was the large, rectangular basilica for official, public liturgies, and there was the shrine containing the tomb of Christ for the private devotion of the pilgrims. They were separated from each other by a courtyard about one hundred feet across, embodying the belief that they were separate and distinct functions. Each function was very real and very important, but they were different. As we noted above, the hillock of flawed stone found in one corner of the courtyard was not made as central as the tomb because, in the eyes of the people of the time, what was most important was the empty tomb, the symbol of the risen Christ.

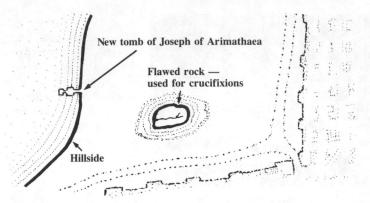

The limestone quarry outside the northwestern walls of the city.

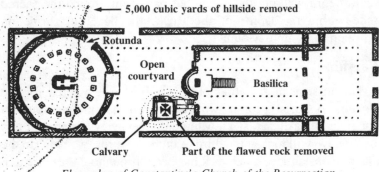

Floor plan of Constantine's Church of the Resurrection

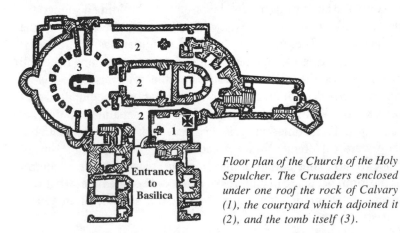

Floor plan of the Church of the Holy Sepulcher. The Crusaders enclosed under one roof the rock of Calvary (1), the courtyard which adjoined it (2), and the tomb itself (3).

Interestingly enough we find this very same arrangement of shrine and public basilica on the Temple Mount. The most imposing building there is the octagonal Dome of the Rock, the shrine containing the rock which Islamic traditions associate with Abraham and Mohammed. This shrine is visited by thousands of pilgrims. Then, a hundred feet or more from the shrine, there is El Aksa, the rectangular mosque used for public worship and considered by Moslems to be their third most sacred mosque.

Scandal

The irreversible change that affected Constantine's church was brought about by historical events explained by the fourth of our key words, scandal. To speak of Jesus as divine, and not just as a holy man, was a scandal. And the streams of pilgrims coming to worship in this blasphemous manner at these blasphemous sites were a scandal to the followers of Mohammed.

They tolerated this scandal for several hundred years in the name of religious peace, even protecting the rights of the Christian pilgrims who came to Jerusalem after the Moslem conquest in 638. But in the year 1009 the fanatical Caliph Hakim decided to crush this scandal. He attacked the Church of the Resurrection, dismantling it, overturning the columns, and disassembling it stone by stone. Then his workers, as we noted earlier, went at the stone of Jesus' tomb with picks and sledgehammers, beating it into rubble.

A few years later, in 1030, the Byzantine ruler Romanus III signed a treaty with the son of Hakim. The treaty gave the Christians the right to rebuild the Church of the Resurrection at their own expense. Money was not available until 1042, when another Byzantine, Constantine Monomachus, arrived and began to work. He rebuilt the rotunda over the tomb in 1048.

When the Crusaders arrived in 1099 they built their church, the one we see today. They roofed in what had been the open courtyard between the basilica of Constantine and the shrine, and included the rebuilt rotunda of Monomachus in their church. What happened to the basilica itself? It has almost completely disappeared, its stones and its location now incorporated into the houses, stores, and streets of the area on which it once stood. The hillock of flawed stone, once in the corner of the courtyard, is now in the

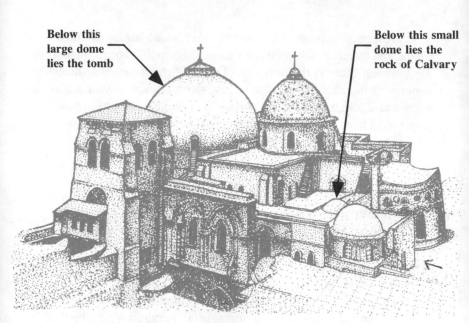

Below this large dome lies the tomb

Below this small dome lies the rock of Calvary

The Church of the Holy Sepulcher seen from the southeast

corner of the church, next to one of the main walls the Crusaders built to support the roof of their church. Since the top of the stone, the place where the Cross was fixed, was the most important part of the stone, a stone platform was built around the top and a low-ceilinged chapel, the Calvary Chapel, built on top of that platform.

Life in the Holy Land

The archaeologists have outlined the traces of Constantine's basilica, its foundation walls and stairways now serving as foundations for neighboring houses. The historians have detailed the course of events that led from the quarry of Herod's time to the church we see today. Religious and biblical scholars have explained for us the changes in religious practice and sensibility that have led different people over the centuries to adapt the buildings to their own use. The only thing that has not changed is the stream of pilgrims, larger or smaller as circumstances dictate, that has come here for nearly two thousand years to do honor to the place of Christ's death, burial, and Resurrection. In the course of our history we will draw on the work of these scholars to explain the politics, economics, religion, culture, and social life of the Holy Land in the time of Jesus. So much has changed that the remains left by the course of two thousand often violent years cannot be properly understood without their help.

Still, we have to be grateful that there are a number of remains. Despite the wars and the destruction, the historical records, in the form of buildings, roads, continuously occupied or abandoned and rediscovered sites, are considerable. The written records are substantial. The amount of archaeological investigation that has been accomplished in the last several generations, and the quality of that work, is extraordinary. With these historical records we can look at the Gospels, place them in their setting, and develop a sense of the way they sounded to the people in Jesus' time.

There are answers to the questions we have about this most important of times. This short history will attempt to give an initial sketch of the Holy Land in the time of Jesus. Admittedly, this short history is only a sketch, a summary, and will not attempt to go into detail. That work is already done, and done well by great scholars. At the end of the history I will add a list of their works that should be available in most libraries for the individuals who want to read further.

Jesus came into an established political and religious world with its own way of doing things. He evaluated what he saw, praising what was good and condemning the evil. He also set the ground-work for major institutional changes, ones which still affect our world. What these changes were and why he brought them about are revealed little by little in the Gospels. But they are revealed often obliquely. Saints Matthew, Mark, Luke, and John wrote to educate specific audiences, and wrote with their audiences' questions in mind. Often the questions are not put the way we would put them. The Gospels do not follow a chronological order, that is, they are not just a history of events listed in their proper order. The events are selected and arranged in order to help the audiences grasp the message of the Gospels. That message is not primarily a historical message.

Today we are more literal-minded. It helps us to know when things happened and why. The following view of the Holy Land will make use of the methods given us by scholars today. They have translated secular and religious writings, pieced together broken tablets, dug through the ruins of ancient Israel, examined and evaluated the fragments of this old civilization, connected them with the monuments that are still standing and, on occasion, still in use, and they have come up with conclusions about life in the land of Christ and in the time of Christ. That is what I hope the reader can draw from this book — a picture of the Holy Land in the time of Christ.

David K. O'Rourke, O.P.

PART ONE:
POLITICAL
BACKGROUND

1
ROMAN POWER IN THE HOLY LAND

"Now at this time Caesar Augustus issued a decree for a census of the whole world to be taken. This census — the first — took place while Quirinius was governor of Syria . . . So Joseph set out from the town of Nazareth in Galilee and travelled up to Judaea, to the town of David called Bethlehem, since he was of David's House and line, in order to be registered together with Mary, his betrothed, who was with child" (Luke 2:1-6).

Saint Luke describes the birth of Jesus within the context of Roman power. How did Rome rule the Holy Land, and how did Roman rule affect the life of the people? What did the Romans control directly, and what was left to local rulers? The power of the Roman Empire is evident in the lives of the people in the Gospels. It is referred to in the teachings of Jesus. Therefore, we will begin our history by describing the influence of Roman power in Palestine.

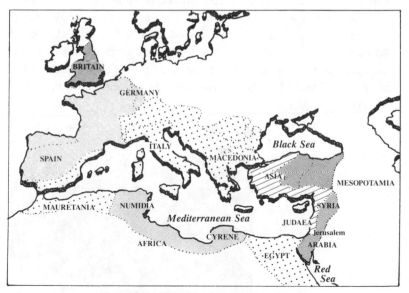

The Roman Empire at the time of Christ

Growth of an Empire

At the time that Jesus was born the Romans were changing from a warlike city-state into the widespread political empire so known to history. They had achieved military control over the lands bordering the Mediterranean a generation before, and now were in the process of consolidating their conquests politically and economically. They planned to transform the conquered countries into Roman provinces. This meant that the defeated countries would accept Roman culture and religion, accept rulers appointed by Rome, support the Roman economy, and be so well integrated into the Roman world that a Roman citizen could go to any of these provinces and feel both safe and at home.

This was the goal, but at the time of Jesus' birth it had not yet been accomplished. The process had begun and was advancing. But the conquered countries, especially those in the Middle East whose culture and history were much more developed than that of Rome, still maintained some autonomy. It was easier for the Roman legions to defeat an army than to subjugate a nation. To bring a defeated nation under their authority the Romans often needed the support of local rulers. In order to get this support they respected local customs and religion and rewarded the local rulers who cooperated with them. And the Romans were usually able to find some native prince who preferred the life of a puppet ruler to the death of a hero. But in those areas that were essential to the maintenance of Roman authority, such as police power and political control, including the power to tax, local autonomy was superficial.

An ancient Roman road that connects the biblical cities of Ai and Michmash

A reading of the history of the times indicates that the Romans did not waste their military resources. They were happy to work through the local rulers who would collaborate with them. This collaboration enabled the Romans to reserve their legions for pushing back the frontiers of the empire and suppressing revolts within it.

The power of Rome was not all that monolithic. There were many quarrels and jealousies in Rome itself. There was bitter class strife, not only between the rich and poor but among the different upper classes as well. Many aristocrats did not view the establishment of an imperial government, that is, rule by a military dictator, with favor. The local rulers in the Holy Land and in the Middle East became good at the game of playing one Roman against another in the attempt to maintain some of their own authority.

Middle Eastern Culture

The area that we know today as the Middle East — Israel, Syria, Jordan, Arabia, Egypt, Turkey, Lebanon, Iraq, and Iran — was the center of the world before and during the life of Christ. Today we often look on these countries as being poor or underdeveloped. But before and during the life of Christ these lands were rich, much richer than Greece or Rome. Middle Eastern culture was flourishing when Rome was just a village. During the generations before the birth of Christ the eyes of Greece and Rome turned toward these Eastern riches. At that time Germany and France and all the countries of northern Europe, countries we think of today as rich and powerful, were unfarmed Ice Age swamps and forests. Economically, it was worth more to the Romans to control the revenues of one good-sized Middle Eastern city than all of France or Germany. The Romans had to subsidize the armies they sent to much of northern Europe, whereas one defeated Middle Eastern ruler could be forced to pay in reparations not only the money it took to defeat him but a sizable, annual tribute thereafter. Today we look on war as a financial disaster. The Romans grew rich on war, especially war in the Middle East.

As the Romans grew from a city-state into an empire and expanded their power into the Middle East they were not moving into a vacuum. They were attempting to conquer ancient, civilized, well-established kingdoms. What today we know only as ruins in the desert or fragments of columns and friezes in museums were thriving cities. Many of these cities are still population centers. The ancient city of Damascus is still the capital of Syria. The city called Rabba in the Old Testament and renamed Philadelphia by New Testament times is today the city of Amman, capital of Jordan.

The Romans were prepared to fight for the land they wanted. This threat of force allowed them to avoid its use and to use intrigue and political skills to exploit the rivalries of the local rulers. Because the rulers were frequently intermarried and because the practice of having several wives created a number of potential heirs (as well as some very bizarre family trees — that is, one of the Herods was his own children's granduncle), the Romans had many jealousies and rivalries to exploit. To the normal history of betrayals, usurpations, murders, incest, and revolution was added the bitterness of family feuding.

Pampered Hostages

The Romans also strengthened their hand through their practice of taking hostages. These were not hostages as we know them, where the individual is kept as a prisoner in painful circumstances. Rather, the hostages were taken from the Middle Eastern royal families, brought to Rome, and exposed to the good life of the Roman aristocracy. Since part of the life of the Roman aristocrat was a close, and frequent, look at the fate of traitors or enemies, the hostages learned to treat Roman rulers with great care. Frequently, as the Romans intended should happen, the hostages were won over to Roman ways. In the event that a throne became vacant, there was always the possibility that the Roman protégé would end up occupying it. Several members of Herod the Great's family spent time in Rome as hostages, and in most cases became advocates of Roman culture and ways.

An important element in Middle Eastern politics before and during the life of Christ was the political power of generals. Roman military leaders were not always motivated by pure patriotism. Military success could be used to build a base for wealth and political power. A tradition coming from the days of the Roman Republic called on the generals to retire humbly and modestly into the background after their victories. However, the

Roman soldiers, as depicted in a bas-relief in the Louvre

generals were often tempted to think that the lands they conquered might just as profitably be governed by themselves as by some friend of the emperor sent in once the fighting was over. The conquered people, especially those with the most to lose such as the royalty or the rich merchants, were certainly going to exploit any and every possible advantage or rivalry which might preserve something of their position and fortune, or at least salvage whatever could be salvaged from the defeat. A general who was more ambitious than loyal could become the obvious hope for salvation.

During the three centuries before Christ the Middle East rarely lived in prolonged periods of peace. War was common. Nations lived with each other either as victors or vanquished. Their borders were secured by defeating the peoples on the other side. Military force was a common and expected means of foreign policy. Diplomacy often meant the ability to turn the enemies of one's enemy into one's friends. A rival power's enemies, no matter whether this meant a neighboring kingdom, an army commander, or an impatient heir, could be wooed and won with arms, gold, or promises of power. It was only later, around the time of Christ's

27

birth, that the *Pax Romana,* or Roman peace that Augustus established throughout the empire, relieved this state of constant warfare.

How did the Romans come into the Holy Land? For all intents and purposes they were invited in. The circumstances of their arrival bring us to the next part of our background, the rise and rule of Herod the Great. It was the family of Herod who profited the most from the arrival of the Romans.

2
KING HEROD
AND HERODIAN POWER

"After Jesus had been born at Bethlehem in Judaea during the reign of King Herod, some wise men came to Jerusalem from the east. 'Where is the infant king of the Jews?' they asked. 'We saw his star as it rose and have come to do him homage.' When King Herod heard this he was perturbed, and so was the whole of Jerusalem" (Matthew 2:1-3).

"When Pilate heard this, he asked if the man were a Galilean; and finding that he came under Herod's jurisdiction he passed him over to Herod who was also in Jerusalem at that time. Herod was delighted to see Jesus; he had heard about him and had been wanting for a long time to set eyes on him . . . " (Luke 23:6-8).

The course of Middle Eastern history enters into the Gospel narratives most directly in the persons of the Herods. From Herod the Great who is mentioned at the birth of Jesus to the Herod who interrogated Jesus a few hours before his crucifixion, the members of this extraordinary family, both men and women, played a major role in the life of all Palestine. Who were they, and where did they come from?

Alexander the Great

The family of the Herods came out of a political situation that began when Alexander the Great and his Greek armies conquered the entire Middle East, including Egypt and Persia and as far east as India. This happened in the year 334 B.C. Alexander died young, but the Greek culture he established remained in these lands up to the time of Jesus. A large percentage of the Jews at the time of Jesus were Greek-speaking. Many lived in the major Greek commercial centers in the Middle East. Chief among these centers was Alexandria in Egypt, founded by and named after Alexander.

Alexander's generals divided his kingdom among themselves after his death. The most important parts of the division, from the point of view of this history, were the provinces of Egypt and Syria. Egypt included present-day Egypt and Libya. The province of Syria included present-day Lebanon, Syria, and part of Iran.

The Greek rulers of Egypt were descended from Alexander's general, Ptolemy. Their dynasty was known as the Ptolemaic Dynasty. Cleopatra, the famous queen of Egypt who at different times lived with Julius Caesar and Mark Antony, was a member of this Greek dynasty.

The Greek rulers of Syria were descendents of Alexander's general, Seleucus. Their family was known as the Seleucid Dynasty. They ruled Syria from the city of Antioch. A glance at a map of the Middle East will show that the Holy Land, or Judaea more exactly, with Jerusalem at its center, is in between Egypt and Syria. It was in between them in more than geography, because these two

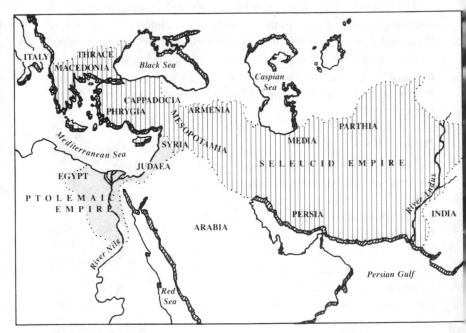

The Greek Empire after Alexander the Great's death (323 B.C.)

30

Greek dynasties were constantly sparring with each other and were frequently at war, trying to expand their frontiers at the other's expense. This battling went on from the time of Alexander's death until Rome defeated each of them before the birth of Christ.

Seleucid war elephant

The rivalries between the Seleucids and the Ptolemaics were exploited by the Romans as they extended their own power into the Holy Land. But before the Romans took full control, and after the two Greek dynasties were weakened by their struggles with each other, with their neighboring kingdoms, and with the growing power of Rome, a Jewish national independence movement managed to begin and succeed. This independence movement led to the rule of Herod the Great.

The power of Herod and his family emerged from a world of warfare, intrigue, assassination, and jealousy centered in Rome. The actors in Rome's strife and jealousies are well known to us. Everyone has heard of Julius Caesar, Pompey, Antony, and Cleopatra. What was Herod's connection with these people? Unless we understand this we will not be able to comprehend how this man who was not really a Jew, who came from pagan roots, who was far from being pious, and who today would probably be considered a dangerous madman, ended up running the Jewish state. There is no doubt that the Roman government and the emperor himself considered Herod a man to be taken seriously. Who was he, and where did he come from?

Idumaea

To the south of Judaea, inland from the Mediterranean Sea at the point where it begins to curve across to the top of the Sinai Peninsula, lies a dry and desolate land. It is part of the desert fought over and occupied by the armies of Israel and Egypt in our

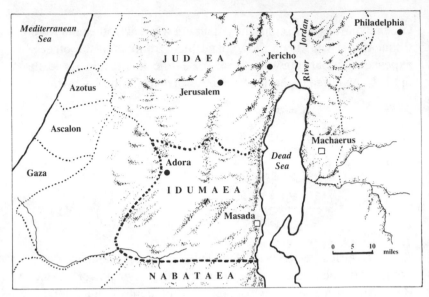

Idumaea, 63 to 55 B.C.

own twentieth century. During the time of Christ it was known as Idumaea, and was a land of nonbelievers. It did not rank high on the list of wealthy or significant nations.

Several generations before the birth of Christ a Jewish leader, Alexander Jannaeus, conquered Idumaea as part of his campaign to establish a free and independent Jewish state. Alexander Jannaeus was exploiting the traditional rivalry between the Seleucid Greeks in Syria, north of Judaea, and the Ptolemaic Greeks in Egypt to the south. Through his war for independence he was able to bring a short-lived period of freedom to the Holy Land. He was more interested in breaking Egypt's military power than in conquering Idumaea, but he couldn't attack the Egyptian borders safely without first securing Idumaea which lay in between Egypt and Judaea. The Jewish leader appointed a local chieftain to be his governor of Idumaea. The chieftain's son was Antipater and his grandson was Herod. Both Antipater and Herod learned well the lesson of political opportunism.

Coin of Alexander Jannaeus

32

Hyrcanus and Aristobulus

The Jewish king, Alexander Jannaeus, had two sons. Their unceasing and unyielding rivalry set the stage for the rise of Antipater and Herod. We mention the two sons because they enter again and again into the history of the times. The older son, Hyrcanus, became the high priest of the Temple in Jerusalem. The younger son, Aristobulus, was jealous of his brother and wanted power for himself. During their father's reign the two brothers kept their feuding under control. After Alexander Jannaeus' death their mother, the queen Alexandra, managed to keep peace between the brothers as long as she lived. But when she died, about seventy years before the birth of Christ, the jealousy and squabbles turned into open warfare. Hyrcanus consolidated his position and declared himself king in addition to being high priest. Aristobulus, who was a better soldier, rose in revolt, deposed Hyrcanus, and named himself both king and high priest.

It was at this point that the family of Herod moved into Palestinian politics — on the wrong side, it turned out, for the first and last time. Down in his Idumaean kingdom Antipater rallied support for the deposed Hyrcanus, and tried to help Hyrcanus to win back his throne by convincing another desert ruler, the King of Nabataea, to lay seige to Jerusalem. Nabataea was a prosperous kingdom of desert people who had made the desert bloom and whose territory, to the south of Idumaea, straddled many important trade routes. The plot to restore Hyrcanus failed when Aristobulus turned to the Roman general, Pompey, for help. Pompey was in Syria to the north, putting the pieces of the Seleucid Empire back together again but in the form of a Roman province. Accustomed to having to fight his way into the Middle East, Pompey was willing to accept the invitation to walk into the Holy Land. Further, the Romans were not happy to see local rulers like the Nabataean king flex their military muscles in areas that they, the Romans, wanted to control. A strong kingdom in Nabataea did not fit in with their own expansionist plans. Rescuing Aristobulus would place him in their debt and under their control, so the Romans came to his aid. They warned the king of Nabataea to lift the seige of Jerusalem and head south again. He did, knowing the consequences should he refuse. In this instance Antipater ended up on the wrong side. That rarely happened again. Antipater learned one of the chief lessons an ambitious politician must learn — to make friends with the powerful. And in his world, power was falling into the hands of Rome.

yeh!

Pompey

In the year 63 B.C. events took a dramatic and terrible turn for the Jews, but a turn which brought Antipater and his son Herod good fortune. The Roman general Pompey had been charged with ridding the eastern end of the Mediterranean of commerce-disrupting marauders, a task he accomplished well. He had come to Damascus in Syria in 66 B.C., just a year before the plot by Antipater and King Aretas of Nabataea to put Hyrcanus back on his throne. He was in Damascus, as we noted, to establish a Roman province in Syria. After he arrived in Damascus the still-feuding brothers, Hyrcanus and Aristobulus, each came to Damascus to try to win Pompey over to his side. Apparently, the belligerent Aristobulus mixed in threats with his arguments and pleas. Pompey took the threats seriously. He set out with his Roman legions for Jerusalem in order to crush the power of Aristobulus. Hyrcanus was already back in Jerusalem when Pompey arrived, and relatively secure in the well-fortified city. However, Hyrcanus, who had learned some political lessons, ordered that the gates to the city should be opened to the Romans in a gesture of submission. Pompey appreciated the gesture. Since Antipater was still at Hyrcanus' right hand we might wonder whether or not this crafty politician was applying some of the hard lessons he had learned previously.

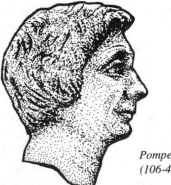

Pompey
(106-48 B.C.)

34

Fragment of the five-foot stone balustrade that marked off the court of the Gentiles and the more inward court of the temple area. The inscription reads: "No foreigner is to enter within the balustrade and enclosure around the temple area. Whoever is caught will have himself to blame for his death which will follow."

After he entered Jerusalem Pompey broke up the fortifications to the Temple. Then, waiting for the right moment, he did something that sent a wave of shock through the people. He went into the innermost, most sacred part of the Temple, the Holy of Holies. For the religious Jew or even the superstitious Jew this would have been the most sacrilegious and shocking of actions. Only the high priest was allowed to enter the Holy of Holies, and then only once a year, on the Day of Atonement. And while the high priest was inside the other priests would wait anxiously outside, hoping that he would come out quickly before something went wrong, causing God's disfavor to fall on them all. For a pagan even to enter the area surrounding the Temple was a crime punishable by death. But for a pagan to enter the Holy of Holies and walk out unharmed, alive, and in control of the city was an event that had happened only a few times before, each one preceding destruction or massacres or exile. Either God was punishing them for some great crime, or the Romans were stronger than God, or all that they had been taught from the beginning of time was untrue. But whatever the explanation might be it seemed that Roman power was not subject to the same limitations that God placed upon their own.

Abomin-
#1

35

Pompey reappointed Hyrcanus high priest and allowed the worship in the Temple to continue. He sent Aristobulus to Rome as a hostage. But the formerly independent kingdom that Alexander Jannaeus had ruled, a kingdom that was as large as the kingdom of Solomon and David, was now reduced to a small territory surrounding Jerusalem.

Off in Rome a series of events unfolded, bringing about the rise of Antipater and his family. Julius Caesar, returning victorious from one of his military campaigns, brought his armies to Rome. Roman law and tradition forbade generals to bring their troops into Rome, as a way of protecting the republic from military takeover. Caesar broke that law, brought his troops to Rome, and began to seize power. The Roman Senate, desperate to preserve the republic, appealed to Pompey to stop Caesar. Pompey, still in the Middle East, agreed, especially since he saw Caesar as a stumbling block in the way of his own ambitions. In retaliation, Caesar sent back to Jerusalem all the Jewish political prisoners and hostages who might make trouble for Pompey. Among the released was Aristobulus.

Caesar's armies left Rome, marched against Pompey's legions in the Middle East, and defeated them. In defeat, Pompey fled to Egypt because the current pharaoh, the boy Ptolemy VII, was his ward (and a brother of Cleopatra). Ptolemy had become Pompey's ward when Pompey was given control of the eastern end of the Mediterranean, including Egypt.

In Egypt, however, a spirit of nationalism was on the rise. The Egyptians had become tired of Roman exploitation and were now on no side except their own. When Pompey landed in Egypt they were waiting for him and killed him.

Caesar was not upset to hear of Pompey's end, but the Egyptians' newfound courage and independence were something else entirely. With the defeat of Pompey, Caesar inherited the responsibility for holding this part of the Roman Empire together. The act that had rid him of a rival and an enemy was also a challenge to his new authority. He was forced to move south to Egypt to suppress any move to independence on the part of the Egyptians and the Ptolemies.

Antipater Helps Caesar

The Egyptians proved to be more serious about their revolt than Caesar had anticipated, and militarily stronger than he had expected. He ended up trapped and cut off in the city of Alexandria. When word of his situation reached the outside Antipater went into action. He dispatched Judaean troops to help Caesar, and he also began an effective campaign in the large and influential Jewish community in Alexandria to win support for Caesar's cause. With this new assistance Caesar was able to crush the rebellion, reestablish Roman supremacy, and strengthen his own personal position.

From this point on Antipater's fortune was tied in with Caesar's. His own star continued to rise as long as Caesar's did; and interestingly enough, Antipater was assassinated shortly after Caesar. Caesar rewarded Antipater for his help in Alexandria. He granted him Roman citizenship, a recognition that carried a stamp of special approval. Antipater's royal ally, the high priest Hyrcanus, was named ethnarch, a recognized title in the empire. Antipater himself was made procurator of the Jewish lands under Roman control, which gave him both civil and military authority within the empire. In addition, the Jewish people were given religious guarantees which continued even after Caesar's death.

It is at this point that Herod enters our history. When Caesar named Antipater procurator he installed his son Herod as military governor of Galilee. At the same time Caesar granted two major privileges. First, taxes were reduced. Considering the subjugating nature of Roman taxation as well as its financial importance, this action had the effect of stimulating a more confident attitude toward trade. Second, and this proved to be a most important and long-lasting benefit, the Jews were granted the unusual right of free assembly in their community centers, called synagogues. As we shall see later on, the synagogue was a relatively new institution, and was becoming the gathering place of the local community. It served as civic meeting hall, religious education center, place of worship, court of law, and financial center. The Romans were usually wary of local institutions that could serve as rallying points of anti-Roman nationalism, so the concession was an unusual mark of favor. The concession meant that the religious and social functions that were part of traditional Jewish life could be continued and even developed. Allowing the freedom of assembly within the synagogue not only granted the people a sense of autonomy but did so in a way which strengthened the traditional religious roots and practices.

Two hundred years earlier the Seleucid Greeks were trying to do just the opposite. As we shall describe later, they were trying to Hellenize the Jews and suppress traditional Jewish ways. They tried to do away with Jewish public places in favor of the Greek public places, like the gymnasium, the theater, the stadium, and the temples of the Greek gods. Seen in this context, Caesar's action was a welcome support for Jewish life. As we shall see, it strengthened the hands of the Jewish moderates who were trying to work out an accommodation with the Greco-Roman world.

With the assassination of Julius Caesar in the year 44 B.C. Herod found himself put to the test. His own father, Antipater, was murdered several months later, and the subsequent years were ones of turmoil. Herod was driven from Jerusalem by an army of invading Parthians, who were trying to stop the spread of the Romans into the territory of the old Persian Empire. The Parthians were the rich and powerful rulers of that part of the Middle East that lay beyond the Roman boundaries. They controlled the riches the Romans were after, were a strong power in Middle Eastern politics, and were successfully able to limit Roman power to the western edge of the Middle East. They were natural allies for an anti-Roman Middle Eastern rebel or ruler.

Herod: King of Judaea

These Parthians formed an alliance with the son of Aristobulus, Antigonus. Their hope was to win the native Palestinian aristocrats into an anti-Roman league. When the Parthians invaded Jerusalem Herod fled to Rome to seek safety and support for his cause. In Rome the Senate, along with the new dictators Antony and Octavian, Caesar's nephew who later became the emperor Augustus, named him King of Judaea. This was not as magnanimous an action as first it might seem. Herod was in exile in Rome. Antigonus was safely in the royal palace in Jerusalem. All Herod received, in effect, was permission and blessing to wage a war against Antigonus to win a kingdom for himself and for Rome. It took three years of warfare to overthrow Antigonus, but it was a fairly complete victory.

Execution after execution followed the victory. The Jewish royal family, the descendants of the Maccabees and of Alexander Jannaeus, were all but done away with. Forty-five members of the chief priestly families who also belonged to the Sanhedrin were executed. Herod made it very clear how he was going to handle opposition. To settle the recurrent question of his own political legitimacy — like Antipater, he was still looked on as being an Idumaean outsider and no real Jew — he married Mariamne, a granddaughter of both Aristobulus and Hyrcanus. Through this marriage he made himself a member of the Hasmonean family.

Herod became king effectively in 37 B.C. and ruled for thirty-three years. His rule was memorable. The first ten years were spent in consolidating his rule. In the concrete this meant putting to death all those who might be in a position to conspire against him. Not only did this mean his traditional enemies, the conservative aristocrats and the members of important priestly families, but it included members of his own family as well. First to be mentioned is his wife Mariamne, one of his ten wives. On one of his trips abroad he left word that if he were to fall into the hands of assassins she was to be killed to prevent her from falling into the hands of his enemies. She apparently found this thoughtfulness somewhat less than comforting, and said so to people in the court. Having been raised a Hasmonean princess she thought her displeasure important. It was not, at least not to Herod. He found it seditious and had her executed.

It was at this time, also, that Antony and Cleopatra tried to establish their own Hellenist empire based in Alexandria. Antony and Octavian had been co-governing the empire since Caesar's assassination, but each of them was also trying to gain a situation of undivided power. Antony decided that with no real power base in Rome he would set up his own kingdom, controlling the eastern end of the Mediterranean. In the meantime, however, he was still a legitimate Roman commander and had the right to demand obedience from Herod, who was subject to the Roman leader in the Middle East.

Mark Antony   Cleopatra

henf conb

Mariamne's mother, a close friend of Cleopatra, was more than willing to urge Antony and Cleopatra to demand signs of submission from her son-in-law, whom she detested. As long as the two were in power she could do so safely. But with Antony's break with Rome, his war of rebellion, his defeat, and the deaths of the two lovers, Herod was able to give vent to his well-nursed desire for vengeance and put his mother-in-law to death. Events such as this left the Jewish people with a distinct distaste for Herod, a distaste that never fully went away. It was offset somewhat by the next period of his life, a dozen years of monumental building.

Herod: Master Builder

During these years Herod set about the building program that brought him fame throughout the Roman world. He created prosperity, and he taxed the prosperity he created. He was interested in promoting commerce, and to this end he established new trading centers. He also fortified the existing trade centers to make them safe from raiders. In addition, he built ports like the magnificent city of Caesarea Maritima, defended caravan routes against brigands, and supported new commercial ventures. Under Herod the commerce in the kingdom reached a level of prosperity it had not enjoyed for many years, a situation we will examine in detail in our chapter on Palestinian economics.

One of the two Roman-style aqueducts built by Herod the Great at Caesarea Maritima, or Caesarea-on-the-Sea, to honor Augustus Caesar. These aqueducts supplied water from the springs of Mt. Carmel, seven to ten miles away.

The Western or Wailing Wall — the retaining wall on the west side of the Temple Mount. Some of these limestone blocks are colossal in size and weight. (The largest one is over 46 feet long and has an estimated weight of more than 400 tons.) The average block is about 12 feet long and about 3½ feet high. The typical masonry of this period showed a flat frontal surface that was "marginally drafted," that is, with a narrow lip chiseled around the edge.

This commercial success created the new revenues that paid for his famous public works projects. He employed thousands and thousands of men in these undertakings, and won the approval of the people because of his generous wages and prompt payments. The grandeur of his buildings increased the awe in which he was held. His reconstruction of the Temple in Jerusalem brought him the greatest recognition and approval. Considering that he also raised temples to pagan gods, he did well to offset this impiety with his efforts in Jerusalem. Even in Jerusalem, though, his actions offended the pious, for he placed a golden eagle, the symbol of the sun god, over the entrance to the Temple. This idolatrous symbol, doubly evil because it was both a graven image forbidden in the Law of Moses and an image of a false god, was a constant affront to the religious people who had to pass under it when entering the Temple. It is also a good indication of Herod's own ambivalent and peculiar nature. The symbol was finally torn down by young disciples of the Pharisees in a protest that started an armed revolt against the Romans.

Herod had been clever enough to win and maintain the support of Octavian, who emerged from his battles with Antony as the Emperor Augustus. Considering the shifting nature of Middle Eastern and Roman politics, this was an accomplishment. But

The Temple with the golden eagle

The Roman forum of Sebaste (Greek for Augustus). The stately columns themselves probably date from the Second Century A.D., but the original foundation of the forum is from the Herodian period. In this rebuilt Samaritan city Herod married one of his wives and murdered two of his sons.

Herod's own heirs were not as fortunate. Herod lived in constant fear that his power would be taken from him again, and he suspected conspiracy in every corner of his palace. In time he became truly paranoid, even to the point of having his own sons executed. Alexander and Aristobulus, Hasmonean aristocrats through their mother, Mariamne, were put to death several years before Herod died. With the Hasmonean princes out of the way, his oldest son by his first marriage, Antipater, stood to inherit the throne. But when Antipater began acting like a king just a few days before Herod's death, the jealous king had him, too, executed. His kingdom was divided in his will between his sons Philip, Herod Antipas, and Archelaus, who were faced with Rome's expanding power. As we will now see, the way they ruled their territories affected the life and teachings of Jesus.

3
THE LATER HERODS

"When Pilate heard this, he asked if the man were a Galilean; and finding out that he came under Herod's jurisdiction he passed him over to Herod who was also in Jerusalem at that time" (Luke 23:6-7).

"It was about this time that King Herod started persecuting certain members of the Church. He beheaded James the brother of John, and when he saw that this pleased the Jews he decided to arrest Peter as well" (Acts 12:1-3).

"Some days later King Agrippa and Bernice arrived in Caesarea and paid their respects to Festus" (Acts 25:13).

The rulers mentioned above are all descendants of Herod the Great, and they are all different. The two Herods mentioned are not the same person. Who were they, how were they related, and what was their influence on the life of Jesus and the early Church? Their stories are involved and historically very interesting. They did affect the life of the Church in a very real way. We shall touch on them where they affect the life of Christ and his followers.

The Kingdom Divided

In his will, Herod the Great divided his kingdom between his three sons, Archelaus, Philip, and Herod Antipas. The transfer of power illustrated the way Rome used such situations to increase its own authority without any extra use of money or of Roman legions. As we shall see at the end of this section, it also clarifies one of the most puzzling parables in the Gospels.

Herod had planned to name his son Herod Antipas king in his own place, but shortly before his death he changed his mind and assigned him only Galilee and Perea. These territories were considered to be of secondary importance. To his son Archelaus he gave the territory of Judaea, Samaria, and Idumaea, along with the title of king. This territory included Jerusalem and the greater part

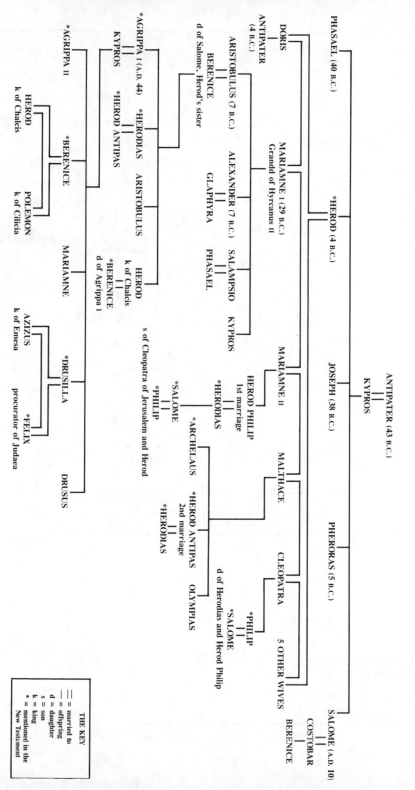

A PARTIAL GENEALOGY OF THE FAMILY OF HEROD

THE KEY
== = married to
|| = offspring
s = son
d = daughter
k = king
* = mentioned in the New Testament

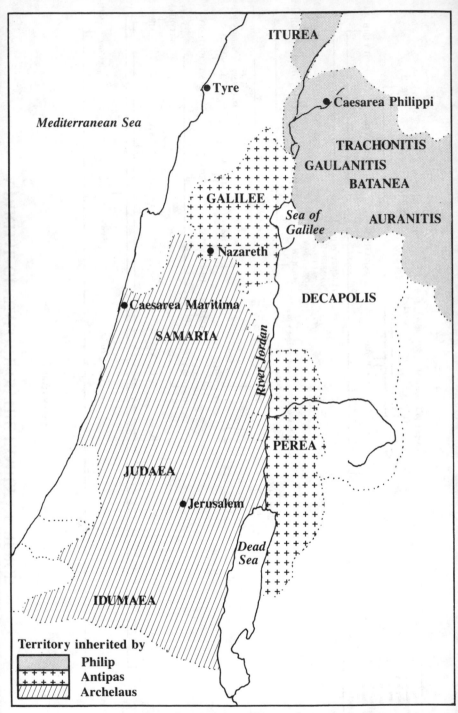

Herod's kingdom divided among his sons

of the Holy Land from the Jordan Valley to the Mediterranean Sea. It was by far the lion's share of the division, and Archelaus turned out to be very much the lion. Philip was given the northernmost provinces of Herod's kingdom: Iturea, Trachonitis, Gaulanitis, Batanea, and Auranitis. These were extensive lands, some of them prosperous, but they were removed from the center of Jewish life and were not part of the traditional Jewish kingdom. Philip and Herod Antipas were each given the title tetrarch, which means the head of a fourth part.

Archelaus went off to Rome to have his kingship confirmed. As often happened, he did not receive the title. A delegation of citizens from Judaea also went to Rome to plead against his appointment as king, and they were heard. The emperor confirmed Archelaus in the possession of his lands, but stripped him of his title. He was not to be king but only an ethnarch, which means head of the people. It lacked the royal symbolism and power associated with being a king. Implicit in this denial was the statement that the only king was Caesar. Archelaus proved to be such a tyrant and so cruel that even the Romans could not tolerate his government and deposed him in the year A.D. 6.

The fact that a delegation of citizens from the Holy Land went off to Rome to plead their case against his appointment as king strengthened Roman power in Judaea. With each side seeking Roman approval and support, the real winner, just as it had been when Hyrcanus and Aristobulus appealed for the same support, was Rome itself. After Archelaus was deposed and sent into exile, to Lyons in France, the Romans appointed their own administrator for Judaea. Once again the Romans were able to replace a local ruler with their own government by political methods, eliminating the trouble and expense of having to use armed force. They also won the approval of the people for ridding them of a tyrant.

Herod Antipas and Jesus

Herod Antipas, who is referred to in the Gospels simply as Herod, played a major role in the life of Jesus. He was significant for three reasons. He was the ruler of Galilee during the life of Jesus. As such it was he who had the right to condemn or free Jesus. To make friends with Pontius Pilate, Herod sent Jesus back to the Roman after Pilate deferred to him. Second, it was he

*Coin of Herod Antipas,
struck at Tiberias*

who condemned John the Baptist to death and ordered his execution. Third, it was he who married his brother Herod Philip's wife, Herodias. It was the dance of Herodias' daughter, Salome, that caused Herod Antipas to promise her anything, a promise she used to call for the head of John the Baptist. Eventually, Herod was deposed by Caligula and exiled to Vienne, in the center of France.

Philip the Tetrarch

The third of the rulers, Philip the Tetrarch, does not enter into our history, other than that he married Salome, the daughter of Herodias and Herod Philip.

Philip died without an heir, and the Emperor Tiberias joined his territory to the Roman province of Syria. Once again the Romans used a peaceful occasion to extend their direct control over territory that had been part of the Jewish kingdom of Herod the Great.

People often find it difficult to keep the members of this family separate one from the other. This is understandable. Herod the Great had ten wives. His first queen, the Hasmonean princess whom he had murdered, was Mariamne. His second queen was also called Mariamne. Herod's oldest son, Aristobulus, whom he executed a few days before his own death, was the father of Herodias. She was first married to Aristobulus' half-brother, Herod Philip, then to his other half-brother, Herod Antipas. Herodias and Herod Philip had a daughter, Salome, who was married to the fourth half-brother, Philip the Tetrarch. This means that Philip the Tetrarch's wife was also his niece and his great-niece, since she was the daughter of one of his brothers, the granddaughter of another brother, and his own father's great granddaughter.

The Two Agrippas

The last of the Herods to be identified are mentioned in the Acts of the Apostles. In one place, at the execution of James, the king is called Herod. In another, at the arrest of Paul, he is called Agrippa. Who were they? They are kings Herod Agrippa I and Herod Agrippa II, father and son. The father, Herod Agrippa I, was the son of Aristobulus and grandson of Herod the Great and his Hasmonean queen, Mariamne.

The family traditions did not change in these later generations. Herod Agrippa I had five children. His daughter, Berenice, lived with her brother, Herod Agrippa II, for a while, causing quite some gossip. She married her father's brother, Herod of Chalcis, and later on became the mistress of the general and emperor, Titus. His troops destroyed Jerusalem, leveled the Temple stone by stone, and slaughtered the population, in A.D. 70.

The southwest corner of the Temple Mount, showing recent excavations. When the Roman troops destroyed the Temple in A.D. 70, they carried the building blocks to the edge of the walled-in esplanade and threw them over. The archaeologists have left these stones lying just where they found them, where they were thrown by Titus' troops.

↓ pushed off?

49

A Puzzling Parable

Earlier we mentioned that we would use this history to explain one of the more puzzling parables in the Gospels. This is the parable about the ruler and the money he gave to each of his followers. We will quote the parable and then point out the meaning.

A man of noble birth went to a distant country to be appointed king and afterwards return. He summoned ten of his servants and gave them ten pounds. "Do business with these" he told them "until I get back." But his compatriots detested him and sent a delegation to follow him with this message, "We do not want this man to be our king."

Now on his return, having received his appointment as king, he sent for those servants to whom he had given the money, to find out what profit each had made. The first came in and said, "Sir, your one pound has brought in ten." "Well done, my good servant!" . . . Next came the other and said, "Sir, here is your pound. I put it away safely in a piece of linen because I was afraid of you; for you are an exacting man: you pick up what you have not put down and reap what you have not sown." "You wicked servant!" he said "Out of your own mouth I condemn you . . . " And he said to those standing by, "Take the pound from him and give it to the man who has ten pounds." And they said to him, "But, sir, he has ten pounds . . . " "I tell you, to everyone who has will be given more, but from the man who has not, even what he has will be taken away" (Luke 19:12-17,20-22,24-26).

Like the nobleman in the story, Archelaus went off to a distant country, to Rome, to be appointed king after the death of his father. A delegation of his countrymen also went, to intercede with Caesar in the hope of having Herod's will set aside. Augustus, as we know, appointed Archelaus ruler (ethnarch) but did not appoint him king.

The presumption in Middle Eastern politics was that the man who went off to have his power confirmed was not certain of ever returning. Either assassins could follow him and finish him off along the way, or his enemies would get to the overlord and win their case against the presumptive ruler. To bet on this man would not be to bet on a winner, it would be to take a serious risk. The clever man is the man who waits and watches, sees who emerges from the power struggle, and then throws his support behind the new ruler immediately.

nke

Augustus Caesar, first Roman emperor (63 B.C.-A.D. 14), grandnephew and adopted son of Julius Caesar. He would not allow Archelaus to be king but made him ethnarch. He is mentioned in Luke 2:1 as ordering the census which brought Mary and Joseph to Bethlehem to register.

This parable presupposes that the people listening would be familiar with the story of Archelaus and would be familiar with the political realities in their own country. The man who goes off and buries his money is being clever. No one knows what side he is on, he has taken no sides, and has made no enemies. Should the nobleman not return, and that would be possible, he would keep the hidden money for himself. Further, should some enemy of the nobleman take power and begin his reign by rounding up the nobleman's friends, as Herod the Great did, the man could point to the fact that the pound was wrapped in a napkin and buried in the ground. That was the rabbinically accepted way of saying, "I have nothing to do with this man or with his money."

On the other hand, the man who takes the pound and invests it in the name of the nobleman is being very foolhardy. He has taken a public stand, everyone knows whose side he is on, and he has presented himself as the absent nobleman's aggressive supporter. If the nobleman's enemy comes to power, as often happened, he would be one of the first to go.

The point being made in this parable is that Jesus is asking his supporters to be for him even to the point of foolhardiness. He is telling them that he wants them to be visibly and publicly on his side, even when it is not expedient to do so.

Herod and his family were prime examples of the way in which the culture and standards of the Greco-Roman world had come into conflict with traditional Jewish life and values. The Herods did whatever was necessary in order to assure their position, power, and wealth. They typified the evil use of power and money so often condemned in the Gospels. We will see the dimensions of this cultural conflict and the problems that came with it when we look at the economics and culture of the Holy Land in subsequent sections.

PART TWO:
CULTURAL
BACKGROUND

4
HELLENISM AND JEWISH LIFE

"Now there were devout men living in Jerusalem from every nation under heaven . . . Parthians, Medes and Elamites; people from Mesopotamia, Judaea and Cappadocia, Pontus and Asia, Phrygia and Pamphylia, Egypt and the parts of Libya round Cyrene; as well as visitors from Rome — Jews and proselytes alike . . . " (Acts 2:5,9-11).

The Holy Land in which Jesus lived and taught was no longer a Jewish land. True enough, the people thought of themselves as Jews, as the descendants of Abraham. They worshiped the God of Abraham and Isaac and Jacob, and they tried, to a greater or lesser extent, to keep the Covenant God had made with them. But in many ways the traditional Jewishness of their ancestors was largely a memory. It was no longer what they liked to think of as the land of King David and Solomon, the land of the prophets; no longer a land where, as in the time of Judas Maccabaeus, fidelity to the law was more important than life itself.

A Greco-Roman Colony

What had happened? The Greeks had taken over. The world had moved in on them, the world under the banner of Hellenism. *Hellas* is the Greek word for Greece, and so Hellenism can be understood to mean "Greek-ism." Militarily, economically, educationally, culturally, and administratively the Holy Land in the time of Jesus was a Greco-Roman colony. Jesus probably spoke Greek. His followers would have spoken Greek because Greek was the business language in Galilee. Saint Matthew would have needed Greek to handle the customs office in Capernaum. Saint Peter would have needed Greek to handle the buying of supplies and the selling of fish in his work. Greek was the common language spoken by people involved in commerce.

Why had Greek become so important in the Holy Land? As soldiers, as merchants, as administrators, as teachers, and as

An elaborately sculptured capital in the Corinthian style, found at Capernaum's synagogue

philosophers the Greeks were better than the Jews. As a result of this excellence they were able to bring Judaea, along with most of the Middle East, into their sphere of control and cultural influence. True, Roman military might had defeated the Greek armies a few generations earlier, but the Romans had the highest respect for Greek culture and ways. The Roman rulers advanced Greek culture in their own families and throughout their growing empire as much as the Greeks themselves could have done.

For our purposes it is important to know about Hellenism for several reasons. First, it was the chief influence in the Holy Land next to Jewish traditions. Second, the political and religious struggles that shaped the land Jesus lived in were struggles between those supporting Greek culture, the Hellenizers, and those opposed to Hellenism. Third, the political climate and social uniformity brought about by the spread of Hellenistic culture was a key factor in the quick spread of the Gospel and the expansion of the Christian community throughout the Roman world.

Greek culture was not spread only by armed force. Many people looked to the Greeks as the lights of the world and very much the world's future. They were happy to shed their own older, more primitive culture and religion for the more rational Greek ways. Many Jews, especially the upper classes, were weary of fasts, dietary laws, rules about ritual purity, and obsessive laws, and were content to exchange them for the worldly and more fashionable Greek customs and religion. The good life in the cities of the Roman Empire — with its theaters, sports events, gymnasia, and good education — appealed to many prominent Jews who wanted

56

these advantages for themselves and for their sons. The fact that their own royalty had adopted the new ways and yet maintained their official, public adherence to Jewish religion appeared to give both permission for and instruction in the way to adapt to the new Greek culture.

Herod the Great did not scruple about constructing Greek temples for the use of the pagans in his realm. He built a temple to Caesar in Caesarea Maritima. He built another, of a white marble that impressed visitors, in Caesarea Philippi. When he rebuilt the Temple in Jerusalem, as we mentioned earlier, he put a golden eagle, the symbol of the sun god, over the entrance.

Herod and his heirs constructed gymnasia, theaters, and stadia; and in other ways showed an active appreciation of Greek life and culture. The citizens of these Jewish lands had only to look to their own leaders to see examples of men and women deeply influenced by Greek culture.

The Religious Jew and Greek Culture

For the religious Jew the problem with Greek ways was that they involved idolatry. You did not take part in sports events without offering worship to the Greek gods of athletes. You would not attend classes without offering obedience to the gods of the school. You could not accept an important governmental post without making some kind of knee bend before Caesar that would look and feel somewhat religious, given the Roman connection between imperial authority and religion. The common phrase, "divine Caesar," was a calculated connecting of religious belief with political power.

True, Greek and Roman religion did not have the personally involved, committed quality of Israel's monotheism and Israel's Covenant with God. The Greeks found Jewish religious zeal to be foolish and fanatical. But the Greeks themselves were equally demanding about loyalty to culture and country. They might have demanded little in the way of religious obedience, but the Jews' refusal of even that little seemed seditious. If the Jews would not follow the Greco-Roman custom of casting those few grains of incense on the coals in homage to gods and emperor the way that everyone else did, could they be trusted to be true supporters of Greco-Roman interests?

A carving of the sun god in the ruins of a synagogue in Chorazin. This demonstrates the extent of Greek influence in Jewish life.

Greek culture was not all that religious, at least publicly, but it placed a high value on loyalty and obedience to country. The Roman and Greek rulers wanted some sign of that loyalty from the Jews. The problem was that, for the Jews, this political action of expressing loyalty to the rulers seemed to be religiously compromising.

For the pious Jew an act of political support for a Greek ruler seemed like apostasy. What was especially offensive to these pious Jews was that so many of their countrymen made this act of political support voluntarily. To capitulate under threat of death was one thing, but to do so for reasons of convenience or social advancement was terrible beyond belief. But terrible or not it was common. It was especially common in the Diaspora, the Jewish communities outside the Holy Land. Here the compromise of Jewish religion, at least the religion viewed by the older standards, was the accepted pattern.

To understand the appeal of Hellenism we have to grasp the advantages that went with Greek culture. They were very real. They included peace, prosperity and capitalism, a common culture with greater ease of transportation between regions, secured borders and military strength, and good education. Many of these benefits were new. They were also sufficiently well-recorded that we can get an idea of the appeal they had. And let there be no mistake — they did have a real appeal to the Jewish people.

58

A Corinthian column among the ruins at Jerash, a town about 37 miles north of Amman. This was the biblical town of Gerasa, one of the "ten cities" of the Gospels (see Mark 7:31).

Welcome Changes

The Greeks first impressed the Jews by their military skills, skills used against the Jews as the Greeks first gained their empire in the days of Alexander the Great. The Greeks were tough and physically well-conditioned fighters. The boyhood spent in physical training and in competitive games produced a young man who could march great distances and use weapons with skill. The Greeks also developed better weapons, better armor, and a sense of military tactics. The skills and tactics we associate with Caesar's legions were Greek developments. In the generations between Alexander the Great and the time of Christ, Jews served as mercenaries in Greek armies and brought their admiration for the Greek military back to the Holy Land with them. Nationalist Jewish leaders saw the imitation of Greek military ways as one means to independence. At least militarily, the Maccabees adopted Greek methods in their fight for independence, ironically a fight against Greek domination.

Hellenism was also spread throughout the Holy Land through the use of Greek financial ideas and procedures. Put simply, the Greeks were capitalists. They were financially sophisticated as

59

well. They understood money and credit as ideas. Today we assume these ideas are a part of all human commerce. But they were not common in Old Testament times. People bartered, and they tithed in goods. Even in the New Testament we read of the ancient practice of presenting offerings at the altar and of tithing in goods rather than the use of money. On the occasion of Mary's purification a pair of turtledoves was presented. Jesus mentions the tithing of dill and cumin and the offering prescribed for the cure of the lepers.

The use of money instead of goods in payment of taxes and debts was relatively recent, but we do read of examples of it. The poor widow whose generosity was singled out by Jesus, when she put all she had in the treasury, used small, copper coins. Every Jewish man had to pay a tax for the support of the Temple, the half-shekel. This tax was relatively recent since the coin, the half-shekel, was relatively new. It was new because coinage was a new idea. The earliest histories in the Old Testament speak of the use of gold and silver in payment of debts, along with sheep and food grains. But just as wheat and barley were measured out, so the gold, silver, and copper were weighed out, not counted. Monetary measurements were measures of weight or quantity. They were not measures of value.

The Minting of Standardized Coins

Then came the use of standardized coinage. The coins were standardized by weight, but the fact that they were officially minted did away with the need to weigh them out each time. They were used in the same way that we use coins and currency today.

Coinage did not become common in the Holy Land until after the conquest of Alexander the Great, around 300 B.C. Control of the currency was part of the economically efficient and standardized trade policies that the Greeks introduced. We need think only of the convenience and order that would come with having the same, standardized coinage throughout the Greek world to understand how this would greatly simplify business affairs. A note of indebtedness for one thousand drachmas would mean the same in Alexandria, in Jerusalem, and in Antioch. This standardization in coinage was one of the chief benefits the Greeks brought to those doing business in their subject lands.

[The minting of copper coins, which were of little value, placed money within the hands of the poor people] This further served to reduce bartering in favor of buying and selling.

The Greeks also drew on the national treasury to develop business. In the case of the Holy Land, this meant using the treasury belonging to the Temple in Jerusalem, as Seleucus IV did in the second century. Ports were built and defended, caravan routes were opened up and provision was made for their defense against marauders, and industries like fishing, fish processing, and salt producing were developed. In short, the Holy Land underwent a period of economic growth that deeply influenced Jewish religion, life, and culture.

When and how did this happen? In broad terms it took place between 300 B.C. and 200 B.C. under the Ptolemies. From 200 B.C. to 100 B.C. the Seleucids built on the basis established by the Ptolemies, but it was the work of the Ptolemies that brought the Holy Land into an economically new world. The development of the Holy Land was part of an extraordinary economic development in Egypt and in the provinces controlled by Egypt's royal family, the Greek Ptolemies. That included Judaea. The Ptolemies were interested in money. They had Egyptian grain to sell, and they tried to squeeze as much profit as possible from their grain and other produce. They were prepared to invest capital to increase their profits. Marshes were drained, new lands cultivated, less productive hillsides were terraced, and better grains developed. This development, which was primarily agricultural, extended to livestock, vineyards, and orchards in addition to farmlands.

To assist in this development the Ptolemies employed Greek merchants, administrators, managers, and tax collectors. In Egypt all land was royal property. The Ptolemies combined this advantageous starting point with the newer Greek managerial skills to create a land that yielded cash crops and taxes for the Greek aristocracy and their Greek agents. While this extraordinary increase in productivity, the equally great increase in the tax revenues that came with the prosperity, plus the system of banking that accompanied it was centered in Egypt, it also affected the Ptolemies' provinces, like the Holy Land. The Jews were involved both in the increased productivity and in the heavier taxes.

Equally important, and in the long run probably more impor-

61

tant, was the development of a large and influential Jewish class that worked side by side with the Greeks. This new class was working with the Greeks at the very time that the Pharisees were washing themselves whenever they came in contact with a foreigner. This new Jewish group developed the synagogue as a Jewish copy of Greek institutions. They also developed a new view of Judaism that was not tied to living in the Holy Land. As we shall see, both the synagogue and the spiritualization of the notion of being Jewish, a notion no longer requiring a religious geography, were important in the spread of Christianity. It is also good to note that Jesus never criticized the Jews who fell short of their religious laws through contact with pagans and foreigners.

Unwelcome Changes

The Ptolemies brought about some unwelcome changes in the administration of the Holy Land. The Jews had experienced local autonomy under the Persians, like Darius, who ruled the Holy Land until their defeat by Alexander the Great. The Jews valued this autonomy, especially the religious freedom that went with it. The change to Greek rule was a disaster, for the change spelled the end of this freedom. The Greeks believed in and established administrative uniformity in their provinces. They were very well versed in governmental theory. The educated among them would have read Aristotle's *Politics* and Plato's *Republic,* and would have discussed the art of government during their education. Now they had the opportunity to put their theories to work. They began in Egypt. They learned fast, moved very systematically, and before long had Egypt subjected to an extraordinary system of local, regional, and national controls. They set up an efficient dictatorship, on a par with the ones we find in the world today.

They extended this control to the provinces, including Judaea; and the Jews soon found themselves chafing under Greek rule. The mountains and deserts of the Holy Land were harder to organize than the Nile Delta, but the Greeks never stopped trying. As a result Hellenistic influence crept little by little into Jewish commerce, culture, education, government, and religion. The Greek system of tax-farming was introduced; and it placed a burden on the people, who were given production quotas. The older, Mosaic law imposed a tithe, a percentage of everything produced. If the

Plato conversing with his student Aristotle (from Raphael's "School of Athens")

production was low, the tithe was correspondingly low. Under the Greeks the people had to meet the quota regardless of how low the production might be.

Hellenistic administration and commerce touched the lives of even the poorest people in the Holy Land, and so made a lasting effect on all levels of Jewish life. Greek education, by contrast, was expressly denied to all but the Jewish elite, and yet this education also affected Jewish life. The essence of Hellenism became concrete in the system of education the Greeks developed for their young men, and many scholars of antiquity suggest that nothing comes quite as close to portraying the Greek ideals and self-image better than their education.

Greek Educational System

Greek education combined a study of Greek letters, discipline, and competition. Education signaled what social class you belonged to. It was limited to members of the upper classes. Jewish education, by contrast, was a study of the Law, as we shall see later on. It was set up to teach youngsters how to understand the Law, how to interpret it, and how to teach it; and it was open to anyone with the time, resources, and talent. At the same age when Greek youths, or Jewish youths in Greek schools, were competing in athletic events and winning praise for their prowess, Jewish students were studying the fine points of ancient laws. Needless to say, the less pious and nationalistic among the Jews thought that the students in the Greek schools were more happily engaged.

63

Another drawing card for Greek education was that it was open to selected Jewish officials. It became the sign, par excellence, of a Jewish family's social position in the eyes of the Greek masters. The Greek system won the approval of many Jews who appreciated the benefits that came with Greek culture. They wanted their sons to have this door to cultural and social advancement opened to them. In order to get it, they were willing to sacrifice some of their own tradition. Through a direct participation in the Greek system for the chosen few, and through an admiration of it by the many, the Greek educational system became another way by which Hellenism took root inside Jewish culture.

Alexandria's Temple

One historical coincidence helped in this process of Hellenization. When the Ptolemies came to power in Egypt, in 300 B.C., they moved their capital from the old Egyptian city of Memphis, far up the Nile, to the new seaport at the mouth of the Nile and thus in the heart of the Mediterranean world. This city was Alexandria, named after the conqueror. The Jewish community in Alexandria, for whatever reasons, had more privileges and influence than was common elsewhere. A rich and influential community, as well as being one of the largest in the Jewish world, it was thoroughly Hellenized from its very beginning. It was also home to a new Jewish Temple, a rival to the one in Jerusalem and religiously illegitimate from the religious purists' point of view. However, this illegitimate temple could boast a legitimate priesthood, since the descendants of the Zadoqite priesthood had fled to Alexandria after being deposed by the Seleucids. And in Alexandria, at the command of the Ptolemies, Jewish scholars had translated the Bible into Greek. This, too, was not allowed by Jewish religious law. As a result of these developments in Alexandria, a real but much less traditional and more progressive and Western form of Hellenized Judaism was born.

Some scholars maintain that the history of the Jews during these years, from the conquest of Alexander to the time of Christ, was a struggle between the "Hellenizers" and the "Judaizers." There is some truth in this, in that many pious Jews saw the influence of Greek culture as a watering down of their religion. But it would also be accurate to say that this period represents the interaction of

64

two cultures, one more oriental and primitive, the other more conscious and rational.

The Greeks and their military and spiritual heirs, the Romans, were the masters of the land. Because they were in the ascendancy their culture became amalgamated with Judaism, just as the Jews living under Greek rule were affected by the Greeks. The effects were real and deep on the Jewish people and on Jewish institutions. The contact between the cultures helped shift the mentality of Judaism from the oriental culture it had been to what it was in the time of Christ, a people with doors open to both East and West.

Greek and Roman cultures were self-conscious. Their intellectuals thought of themselves as intellectuals, they thought about the nature and meaning of thought itself, and about what it meant to be Greek. The earlier Jews, by contrast, were concerned about being Jewish and the social and religious rules that had to be observed in order to be Jewish, but there was not the self-conscious and philosophical reflection on Jewishness that was a mark of Greek culture. With time this changed. The Jewish intellectuals adopted the rational, reflective, self-conscious mentality that was a hallmark of Hellenistic intellectualism but not part of their own Jewish tradition. Another example of Hellenist influence on Jewish life was the development of schools in which the teacher himself was remembered by name and whose teachings were accepted in an

(1) "Absalom's tomb" (First Century A.D.) with Ionic columns; (2) "Tomb of the sons of Hezir" (Second Century B.C.) with Doric columns; (3) "Tomb of Zechariah" (First Century B.C.) with Ionic capitals

65

authoritative way. This, too, was common in the Greek world. We can think of teachers like Socrates and Plato and Aristotle, each of whom had his own followers who remembered and quoted his teachings. This practice had been less common in Jewish education where, out of religious humility, the teachers tended to guard their anonymity.

The very development of education as a value came from Jewish interaction with the Greeks. Jewish leaders, impressed by the extraordinary emphasis their Greek masters placed on educating their own elite, began to develop different kinds of Jewish schools. In part this was a defense against being overwhelmed by Greek learning, in part an alternative to the Greek schools, and in part an enlightened and progressive development of their own religious traditions. Jewish religion was based, principally, on the first five books of the Bible, referred to simply as the Law. This was handed down from generation to generation by a form of oral instruction we will describe later. So, establishing schools to teach the Law did not represent a change as much as a development. However, both the new emphasis placed on education and the classroom method itself came from the Greeks. The intellectual efforts of the Jewish leaders in the Holy Land were nationalistic and religious. The Jewish scholars in the Greek world — for example, the Jewish intellectuals in Alexandria — were more open to a philosophical orientation. In the Holy Land itself there was a much more conscious effort to resist the Greek influence. The leaders of this anti-Hellenist effort used a recalling and a reemphasis of their own history as a people as a primary means to combat Greek influence. The Book of Maccabees is a historical account illustrating a heroic resistance to Greek influence and praising the strict observance of the Law. The Book of Judith, which was composed around the same time, uses a historical analogy, the resistance to an earlier oppressor, as an example of the way the Jewish people were to fight foreign cultural influences. This serves to point out that while some members of the upper classes were won over to Hellenistic ways there was, at the same time, a strong resistance movement among some Jewish religious and intellectual leaders. Even negatively, though, Hellenism had a strong influence here, because if it were not for the Greek pressure these histories may not have developed.

66

5
JEWISH EDUCATION

(handwritten margin notes: "do with children's SS class, maybe")

"I tell you most solemnly,
the Son can do nothing by himself;
he can do only what he sees the Father doing:
and whatever the Father does the Son does too.
For the Father loves the Son
and shows him everything he does himself . . . " (John 5:19-20).

The basic educational methods used in the countries of the Greco-Roman world were the same. In Rome, in Athens, in Jerusalem, and in Nazareth boys were taught using the same methods. What was the system? How did Jesus learn, how was he educated, and how did he go about teaching his followers? Since so much of what he did was teaching, we do well to look at the educational system, for it throws a good bit of light on the Gospels in general and on certain puzzling passages in particular.

The First Task: Memorize

Judaism had words for the written and the unwritten law, just as the Greeks and Romans did. In an era which was not separated from the age of oral traditions by very many centuries the existence of these words is understandable. In Jewish education the basis for study was the written Torah, or the Law, the first five books of the Old Testament. In the Greco-Roman world it was the written classics. But the method for learning them was the same. The first task of the student in each culture was to commit the written word to memory. This was a long, difficult task, but it was the task demanded by the educational system. Roman carvings show the master, birch rod in hand, seated in front of the standing students who are reciting from memory. They also show the birch rod being used on the backs of the students. Even today, in Islamic schools the students are called on to recite the Koran over and over again until they have committed it to memory, and the Islamic master *still* still has the birch rod to assist bad memories.

67

Part of a famous cup painted by Duris (Fifth Century B.C.). In the scene shown, the boy is reading aloud from the papyrus roll held by the teacher. The bearded man on the right is the interested parent.

Until A.D. 70, when the repressions and destruction following the Jewish uprisings of A.D. 66 brought about many changes, it was the custom for young boys to be taught by their fathers. After A.D. 70 the instruction was put in the hands of specialists. In the passage from Saint John quoted at the beginning of this section Jesus is probably alluding to his own education and his memory of Joseph's teaching, just as his apostles would have thought back to their own teachers as he spoke.

Written Hebrew: No Vowels

Jewish education had a few differences. To begin with, education was open to girls as well as to boys. And Jewish boys and girls would have had a much harder task to master in learning the written Torah than their counterparts in Rome and Athens because of one of the characteristics of written Hebrew. Hebrew is written without vowels. Since spacing and punctuation are more modern refinements it was common to run words together in written languages. That alone made the work of picking out the words difficult for a beginning student. But the elimination of the vowels was the major difficulty.

For an example of the difficulty, let us look at the phrase that is used to teach beginning typing students, one that is used because it has all the letters of the alphabet: the quick brown fox jumped over the lazy dog. Run together this would read: thequickbrownfoxjumpedoverthelazydog. Confusing looking, but still intelligible. Remove the vowels and you have: thqckbrwnfxjmpdvrthlzdg. Now that is what Jewish boys and girls had to cope with as they began the process of learning to read and write. Today, written Hebrew is pointed, that is, there is a system of little points or dots next to the letters to indicate where the vowels go and what the vowel sound is. But that system was not used in Jesus' time.

Learning to read, and to remember by heart what you read, was the first subject. The second was learning to translate the Scripture into Aramaic. The work of translation was begun after the student had spent a few years on the basics of reading. These two tasks occupied the students from the age of five years until the age of twelve.

The Writing Board

The father taught by using a pinakus, a writing board. We have an example of the pinakus in the story of John the Baptist. Recall that his father, Zechariah, was a priest. He received a vision while offering incense in the Temple that he would become the father of a son. Because he doubted the vision, for he and his wife were old, he was struck dumb. One did not doubt God's promises. When John was born and it was time to name him, his mother, Elizabeth, said that he should be named John. That was not a family name, and the guests said that it was not right to use a non-family name, but they said that his father should decide. Since he was still unable to talk, Zechariah sent for a pinakus, a writing board, and wrote the name John on it. It is quite possible that the pinakus was there for the child's lessons. Even though he was just born, his proud mother and father had already gotten together the boy's school supplies. This, by the way, says something about the value placed on education in the Holy Land.

The task of the five- to twelve-year-old was to learn to read and write and, also, to commit the Scripture to memory. This memorization is called the mishnah. There was a common rabbinical saying, which Saint Paul quotes, "The letter kills but the spirit gives life." This saying refers to the practice of learning the Scripture by heart and being able to quote it without using the text. The written Scripture was dead, but the memorized and quoted Scripture was alive. As a way of emphasizing the importance of memorizing the Scripture the students were not allowed to use written notes. This was also true of classical education in Rome and Athens. It was also true in the synagogue service. Written Hebrew was sufficiently different from the spoken language that it would not be understood by the people who had not had an education. Many poor people were not able to follow the Jewish educational ideal, so there was someone there to translate into the spoken language. But the translator could not use notes, and there was no translation of the Scripture into the modern language. The only written Scripture was the ancient Hebrew text which had to be translated and commented on from memory.

A Son of the Law

At the age of twelve a boy was bar mitzvah, that is, a son of the law and a man in his own right. At this point it would be permissible for his education to end. He was now both permitted and encouraged to take his place in the religious discussions of his elders. At twelve we find Jesus in the Temple discussing with the teachers of the Law. That was where he belonged, both by right and by duty. It was the practice in discussions to let the youngest speak first, and then each one in turn up to the leading priest, who spoke last. What was extraordinary, as the Gospels record, was not the fact that Jesus was in the Temple but the quality of his learning.

It is probable that after the age of twelve Jesus went on to the next level of education. Since Nazareth was small he would probably have gone to a larger town. Sepphoris, the ancient capital, was within easy walking distance from Nazareth, for a strong boy, and would have been large and important enough to have a school. Sepphoris would also have been the location of a very grim lesson that Jesus would have learned in his youth. There was an insurrection there when he was a boy, and the Romans had all the insurrectionists, a sizeable portion of the male population, crucified on the trees surrounding the town.

Higher Education

The higher level of education covered three subjects: the midrashim; the halakot; the haggadot. The midrashim comprise the texts of the Bible, along with all the interpretations and stories coming from the unwritten tradition that go along with the Scripture. We have our own New Testament midrashim, such as the stories about the parents of Mary, Anna and Joachim, who are not mentioned in the Scripture but are part of the unwritten tradition.

The halakot are catechetical or juridical statements, and are what now go to make up the Talmud, the body of law studied by rabbinical scholars. The haggadot are the nonlegal traditions, such as the story of the Passover. They are akin to our liturgical rites. The purpose of studying the haggadah is to gain the ability to tell the traditional story as well as possible, both for the storyteller's benefit and that of his audience. In the course of mastering these three areas the student would first commit the information to memory. Then he would learn how to interpret what he had learned. If a student was able and had the financial resources, he could then go on to an even more advanced school. These were ordinarily located in Jerusalem and prepared the country's religious elite.

"Hook" Words and Phrases

One of the subjects the student at the higher level had to learn was the use of "hook" phrases. This is similar to but not the same as "key" phrases we might use to unlock a part of our memory. The student in Jewish education had a somewhat different approach. He was not looking to unlock his memory; rather, he hung things he wanted to remember on hook phrases.

The hook phrase is not logically connected to the other things hanging from it. It is not the content that is connected. The connection is verbal; it is a system of memorization using similar words. We have several examples in the Gospels. In the parable of the unjust steward we read at the end, "The master praised the dishonest steward for his astuteness" (Luke 16:7). Then there is added the phrase, "For the children of this world are more astute in dealing with their own kind than are the children of light" (Luke 16:8). What does this last statement have to do with the parable? It does not seem to be connected at all. But there is a verbal connection, the use of the word astuteness. Saint Luke, who gives evidence of being especially well-trained in the educational system of the Greco-Roman world, could have put this statement of Jesus at the end of the parable almost by second nature.

There is the example, also, of the wine and the wineskins mentioned in the question of fasting. In Saint Luke we hear Jesus say: "No one tears a piece from a new cloak to put it on an old cloak . . . And nobody puts new wine into old skins; if he does, the new wine will burst the skins and then run out, and the skins will be lost. No; new wine must be put into fresh skins" (Luke 5:36-38). This is how Matthew and Mark have it as well. But then Luke adds: "And nobody who has been drinking old wine wants new. 'The old is good' he says" (Luke 5:39).

What does this phrase have to do with the parable? Nothing, really. It is not connected logically or from the point of view of the sense of the parable. But there is a verbal connection; it talks about new and old wine. Why connect it verbally and place it here? Because that is the way the rabbinic student learned to connect things. In the process of trying to commit all the interpretations of the Law to memory, a mammoth task, the students needed ways to help them memorize these statements. These hook words and hook phrases, on which to hang all the rest, were helpful aids to memorization.

We have an example of the idea of a hook word itself in Saint Matthew. Recall that the Pharisees put a question to Jesus about the greatest commandment of the Law. Jesus replies: "*You must love the Lord your God with all your heart, with all your soul,* and with all your mind. This is the greatest and the first commandment. The second resembles it: *You must love your neighbor as yourself.* On these two commandments hang the whole Law, and the Prophets also" (Matthew 22:37-40). Here Jesus is using a phrase that would have been very familiar to the student.

Jesus probably taught his own followers using the methods we have described. Scripture scholars speak of a period during the ministry of Jesus which they call the "formation of the apostles." What Jesus would have been doing was teaching them so that they could teach others. How would he have taught them? Quite possibly in the way described above. It was the way he and everyone else learned in the Holy Land. In the schools in Jerusalem it was the task of the students to "Learn the mind of the master." That was the mark of the Talmudic scholar. In the same way the apostles would have learned the teachings of Jesus so that they would have been able to pass them on to others.

PART THREE:
RELIGIOUS
BACKGROUND

6
TEMPLE WORSHIP

"Just before the Jewish Passover Jesus went up to Jerusalem, and in the Temple he found people selling cattle and sheep and pigeons, and the money changers sitting at their counters there. Making a whip out of some cord, he drove them all out of the Temple, cattle and sheep as well, scattered the money changers' coins, knocked their tables over and said to the pigeon-sellers, 'Take all this out of here and stop turning my Father's house into a market' " (John 2:13-16).

Jesus disrupts the work of the money changers and drives the sheep and cattle from the Temple. This expulsion of the animal merchants and money changers would have surprised those who saw it. The Jewish worshipers and pilgrims coming to the Temple expected to find animals and money changers in the Temple area. Why? To understand, we have to go back to the roots of worship in the Old Testament. We have to go back to the practice we know as sacrifice, especially the sacrifice of living animals.

Blood Sacrifices

We speak of making sacrifices, by which we mean either giving up something for a higher purpose or doing something difficult for our own sake or for the benefit of others. But killing an animal or a person as an act of worship, that kind of sacrifice we are happy to leave in anthropology textbooks. Yet, at the very heart of Old Testament worship, the worship that took place every single day in the Temple in Jerusalem during the life of Jesus, is this foreign practice of offering the life of a living thing as an act of reverence for God. In the Old Testament we read of instances when one or another of the patriarchs offered a sacrifice. This involved killing a bull or a ram or a goat and, usually, burning the animal's body. The Passover, which was the most sacred of the Jewish feasts, was centered on sacrificing a lamb and then eating that lamb as a sacred meal.

This kind of sacrifice, which is called blood sacrifice, is obviously foreign to us today and seems barbaric. Nonetheless, it was common in primitive religions. It is a way of recognizing that all life comes from God and that all life really belongs to God. Life is sacred because it comes from God. Blood sacrifice recognizes God's right and power to take back life whenever he wants, with no questions asked, and that humans do well to recognize God's ultimate power.

For a moment, think of a poor shepherd grazing a flock of several dozen sheep and goats in a dry, desert wadi deep in the Negev Desert. From somewhere off in the distance comes the sound of thunder, rolling over the dry hills and bouncing off the rock walls of the wadi. A storm is coming. Or has it already come? If it has, the shepherd might expect any minute to see a wall of water racing down the wadi toward him, a flash flood capable of washing him and his master's flocks all the way down to the Dead Sea. Or if the storm is only on the way, he might flee up the slopes to dry land — but there he would run the risk of lightning striking him or one of the animals. There are powers greater than he at work just over the next hills, and he should do whatever he can to stay on the right side of them.

The owner of the flock has heard the same thunder. Should anything happen to the animals his small fortune would go with them, for they represent all that he has. Perhaps if he offers to the god of the storm the life of his best ram he will spare the lives of the others. A shepherd he can hire for a pittance, but it has taken him years to build up this flock. So he goes off to the hills where the animals are and sacrifices the ram.

A wadi *is a ravine which forms the bed of a stream during the winter, but which dries up in the summer.*

God of Power and Might

A primitive view of God and religion? Yes, a very primitive one. What it comes down to is a form of bribery. But this primitive bribery is basic to the religions that were common in the Middle East. It is basic to the roots of the worship that took place in the Temple in Jerusalem.

The patriarchs, who made use of this worship at least two thousand years before the time of Christ, looked at God with awe, reverence, and fear. They saw their own human limitations; they grasped the power and immensity of God; and, quite literally, they prostrated themselves before him. They also believed that anyone who came into the presence of God would be so overwhelmed by God's power that he would die. Even signs or symbols of God's power were to be feared. If you came too close to them, you would die. This is why the apostles who accompanied Jesus to the mountaintop where he was transfigured threw themselves to the ground in fear when God spoke from out of the cloud. This is why Peter asked Jesus to depart from him after the miraculous catch of fish, when some glimmer of who Jesus might be sank into Peter's head and he realized that he was in the presence of God's holy power. We are accustomed to thinking of God as friend, as support, the one to whom we turn in time of distress and trouble. To the religious person of Jesus' time God was a distant, powerful, almighty force who could be approached only symbolically, fearfully, and distantly. His very presence would overwhelm.

Even today in Jerusalem, at the gates to the esplanade where the Temple once stood, and which today contains the beautiful, golden-roofed Dome of the Rock, one of Islam's holiest shrines, the chief rabbis of the modern state of Israel have placed signs forbidding all people to enter onto the esplanade because of the holiness of the place. On the esplanade once stood the Temple, where only the priests were allowed to go and only in their bare feet. And within the Temple precincts, wherever it was located on the esplanade, was the Holy of Holies, where only the high priest was allowed to go and only once a year at that. These were the instructions given by God and recorded in their sacred writings. Both the Jewish priesthood and the Temple have been gone for two thousand years; but God once called this place holy, and God is to be obeyed.

Temple Worship

This view of God, a view which saw God as being so holy that even his name may not be mentioned, required very special religious practices. If the people saw God as so holy and unapproachable, how did they worship him? Strictly speaking, they did not. The common people did not worship God directly. The priests worshiped God for them and in their name. And the priests worshiped through sacrifice, sacrifice offered at a great distance. Worship took place under very controlled circumstances. The Temple in Jerusalem, with its priests and rituals, provided those controlled circumstances. We will look at some of the rules in the Old Testament for Temple worship so we can see just how controlled and ritualized the worship actually was.

One of the books of the Law, Leviticus, describes the way sacrifice is to be offered. The name Leviticus refers to priestly things because the priesthood was established among the descendants of Levi, the head of one of the twelve tribes comprising the Jewish people. All the priests came from this tribe or clan.

The Tent of Meeting

The rules for worship date from the time when the Jewish people were still nomadic, and presuppose a campground where they lived in tents. The sacrifices were offered near a special tent, called the Tent of Meeting. Moses constructed this tent at the Lord's command after the flight out of Egypt. It was called the Tent of Meeting because it was there that Moses went to talk with God and to receive instructions from him. Significantly, the tent was not placed in the camp but just outside it. Holy places and daily life did not mix.

The tent contained several sacred items. The most important was a gold-covered wooden box called the Ark of the Covenant.

This ark served the double purpose of holding the religious objects considered most holy by the Jewish people and of forming a dais on which a type of throne was built. The throne was composed of outstretched angels' wings made in gold. The throne was to be the resting place of the power of God. Since the Jews believed that God was spiritual and not physical, an extraordinary belief in such a concrete age, we may assume that it was thronelike enough to suggest power but abstract and symbolic enough to make clear that it was not built to support a human.

The box, or ark, was covered with gold inside and out. It was fitted at the corners with rings through which poles could be slipped to carry it from place to place. This was to permit it to be moved without anyone having to touch it. The Bible records an incident when the ark was jostled somehow and began to tip over. A man grabbed it to prevent the fall — and died on the spot. We can imagine how this story, told with dramatic detail to generation after generation of Jewish children, impressed on them the need to keep their distance from sacred places and things.

In addition to the ark with its throne there was a special table, again embellished with gold. This table was equipped with dishes and bowls made of gold. The table also had rings and poles to allow it to be carried without being touched. There was, also, a lamp stand of pure gold much like the candelabrum that is used in Jewish ceremonies today.

These items — the ark, the table, and the lamp — went inside the Tent of Meeting. This tent was made by fencing in a large area

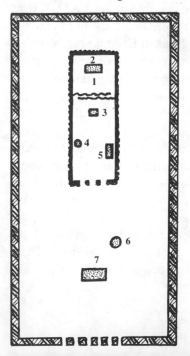

Floor plan for the Tent of Meeting

1 *Holy of Holies*
2 *Ark of Covenant*
3 *Altar of incense*
4 *Golden candlestick*
5 *Table of showbread*
6 *Laver*
7 *Altar of burnt offerings*

79

with linen cloth and putting a goat-hair covering over it. To judge by the directions set down in the Book of Exodus for its construction, it would be similar to the Bedouin tents still in use in the Middle East, but much more artistic and richly made. Inside the tent was a smaller, square area screened in by a purple cloth. This area was called the Holy of Holies. The ark went into the Holy of Holies. The part of the Tent of Meeting outside the Holy of Holies was called the Holy Place. The lamp and the special table went in the Holy Place, along with a small altar for burning incense. Every day a priest, and only a priest, would come into the Holy Place to replenish the supply of oil for the lamp, which was kept burning all the time, and to offer incense on the altar of incense. Once a year, on a day set aside for atoning for the sins of the people, the high priest would go into the inner tent, where the Ark and Throne were, to sprinkle blood as an offering for sin.

The place where the animals were sacrificed was outside the Tent of Meeting. Whether the altar on which their bodies were burned was there as well is not quite clear. By the time the books describing these events were actually written down the people had settled permanently, the nomadic life was only a memory, and the worship itself was set in the permanent buildings of the Temple in Jerusalem. But what is clear is that this sacrifice of animals was important and took place twice a day. The blood of the slaughtered animal was caught in a bowl and then poured out in a special way, offering the blood and the life it represented back to God.

The description of the altar in the Book of Exodus is ambiguous. It is hard to make all the elements in the written description come together into a clear picture. Consequently, we do not know exactly how it looked. However, there were altars for burning sacrificial victims at pagan temples elsewhere in Palestine, and these have been uncovered. What are they like? Imagine a round, stone platform rising about five feet above the ground and about twenty feet in diameter. The platform is made of field stones about the size of footballs. The platform has a set of five or six stone steps cut straight into it, leading from the ground level to the top of the platform.

The Jewish ritual required that a fire be built on top of the platform and that the fire be large enough to consume an ox. There were written specifications for shovels and pans for the ashes. The daily burnt offering, also called a holocaust, was an essential part of Jewish worship in the Temple in Jerusalem up to and during the life of Jesus.

Although blood sacrifice was an essential aspect of Jewish worship, and probably the most significant element in the view of the people, it was not all there was to it. And if worship in proximity to the ark and the Holy of Holies be a sign of importance, the blood sacrifice was not the most important part. The golden table which was used for offerings of bread, the altar of incense, and the lamp stand were right in front of the Holy of Holies. The loaves of bread were renewed periodically, and the incense offered and the light maintained as part of daily worship. This type of ritual envisages a more spiritual and less bloody relationship with God.

The Book of Exodus, with its prescriptions for worship, was compiled under circumstances that may well have colored the emphasis in it. King David captured Jerusalem around the year 1000 B.C., and his son, Solomon, built the Temple there around 950 B.C. It was also at that time, or a little later, that the early books of the Bible were written down. Prior to that time they would have been maintained in unwritten form by men trained from their childhood to remember and retell them.

It was to David's and Solomon's political advantage to have both the Tent of Meeting and the altar used for sacrifice under their control. When David occupied Jerusalem he brought the Ark of the Covenant there. In the nomadic days the Tent of Meeting was set up outside the camp, and while it was outside the camp it was accessible to the people who wanted to visit it. After the move to Jerusalem the Tent of Meeting was no longer outside the camp or

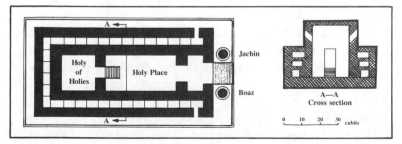

Solomon's Temple

the town. It was adjacent to the house that David built for himself. When Solomon built the Temple he did so in such a way that his own palace was adjacent to the Temple, and his guards could control the Temple. Public access to the Tent of Meeting also disappeared.

David and Solomon wanted and achieved a firmer control of the life and politics of their country than had been common before their time. As part of this control it was to their advantage to control both religious and political authority. So they constructed their palaces adjacent to the Temple in such a way that they were able to control not only the kingship but the priesthood, public worship, and the implements necessary for worship.

The first five books of the Bible, the Law or Torah, were written down, as we noted before, after David and Solomon took charge of Jewish worship. It is probably a safe assumption that when the scribes committed the Bible to writing they did not place too great an emphasis on the access that the people had to the Tent of Meeting in the nomadic days. There is only the simple comment that the "sons of Israel" went to the Tent of Meeting as Moses did. In the Temple only the priests were allowed into the new, permanent "tent of meeting." The scribes could well have said little about their more democratic past because the king's men had reminded them that it isn't always necessary to remember everything.

Herod's Temple

By the time of Jesus, royal control over the Temple was even tighter. Herod controlled the priesthood with an iron hand — a hand which, as the priests well knew, also held an executioner's sword. But the Temple worship continued just as it had in the earlier days. The tents had been replaced by buildings, and in Herod's time by magnificent, new buildings, among the most magnificent in the world. But these buildings were laid out using the same floor plans prescribed in the Bible for the places of worship. The Temple in which Jesus prayed had the same Holy Place with the Holy of Holies inside it. The Ark of the Covenant had disappeared, but there was the altar of incense, the lamp stand, and the table for the loaves of bread. In the area in front of the Holy Place was the altar on which the animals were burned.

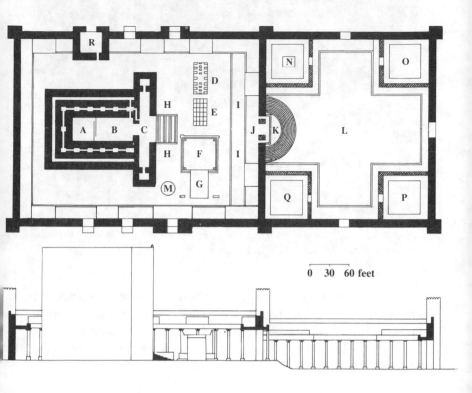

Plan of Herod's Temple

A Holy of Holies
B Holy Place
C Porch
D,E Slaughter places
F Altar
G Ramp
H Court of Priests
I Court of Israelites
J Nicanor's Gate

K Where Levites stood to sing
L Court of Women
M Laver
N Lepers' chamber
O Wood chamber
P Nazarites' chamber
Q Chamber of oils and wine
R Rinsing chamber

These sacred parts of the Temple were not open to the public. Only priests could enter them. In front of the altar area was a forecourt which Jewish men could enter, and in front of that a court open to Jewish women. These areas were all surrounded by a wall, and non-Jews could not enter under pain of death. The area outside the wall was called the Court of the Gentiles. This Court of the Gentiles was by far the largest section, covering about three-

Model of Herod's Temple, built to scale by Professor Michael Avi-Yonah, on the grounds of the Holyland Hotel, Jerusalem

fourths of the Temple area. Not only did it serve as a place for foreigners but, architecturally, it provided a magnificent esplanade from which to admire Herod's buildings. In common speech this entire complex of buildings and courtyards was referred to as the Temple.

Priestly Rituals

The sacrifices in the Temple were carried out by the priests themselves in a ritualized manner. The rituals indicated that God was the source of life and that the life of the animal was being offered back to God. Certain parts of the animal were seen as more connected to life than others. Prime among these were the blood and the fatty parts. We can probably grasp the symbolic role of blood as a life sign, but why the fat was life-connected may be harder to grasp. To understand, we must think of the herds in the Holy Land. In times of drought or famine fat animals survived, whereas thin animals died. The difference between life and death was fat.

In the actual sacrifice the animal's throat was cut, the blood was caught in a basin, and then was poured out in a special way as a sacrifice. The fatty parts were cut out and then placed on top of the altar and burned as sacrifices. In some sacrifices the whole animal was burned. In others the remaining part went to the priests as part of their salary. The priests, incidentally, were said to have had bad

84

A view of the model, showing the upper city in the foreground with the Antonia Fortress and the Temple in the center background

health due to the disproportionate amount of meat in their diet and the fact that they worked all day in their bare feet on the cold, stone Temple floors.

With the large numbers of animals sacrificed in the Temple it obviously became very messy. Part of the priests' work was to keep it clean. In his reconstruction King Herod had provided for water, drains, and sewers to help assure cleanliness.

Another aspect of the blood sacrifice in the Temple was the need for sacrificial victims. Providing these victims was an important part of local commerce. Animals were sacrificed both as part of the official Temple worship and on behalf of individuals, such as pilgrims to the Holy Land, who presented the animals for their own religious reasons.

The Animal Market

As a convenience to worshipers in the Temple, animal sellers had pens full of these animals adjacent to the Temple, even within the Temple precincts. If we can form an image of the animal seller looking for rich worshipers, running through the crowds of people coming into the Temple, and grabbing the potential customer by the arm to see his fine, unblemished animals; if we can form an image of seller and customer haggling over the price, of the animals bleating or bellowing frantically in their pens; if we can imagine the animals being led or dragged and prodded to the altar area to be slaughtered; and all this going on many times over every day, with crowds of people coming, going, and milling around, then we can have an image of what the Temple was like.

This was especially true at Passover. On the occasion of the Jewish Passover people would come from far distant Jewish communities for the celebration and to offer sacrifice in Jerusalem. In addition to their own Passover lamb some pilgrims would arrange to have an additional animal, the larger and more expensive the better, offered in the name of a government official whose favor or approval they were seeking.

At Passover both local Jews and those living in more distant towns in the Holy Land who were able to make the trip to Jerusalem would come to the Temple. Each family would have its animal slaughtered sacrificially at the Temple and would take the carcass to a house or lodging to be prepared for the Passover dinner. How different is this scene — with the smell of animal pens, the screaming of the frightened beasts, the smell of the blood of the hundreds and hundreds of animals spilled out and the acrid stench of burning flesh — from our own notion of worship with its quiet and meditative aspect.

Money Changers

The presence of foreign Jews in Jerusalem accounted for the presence of money changers in the Temple. The Jewish community was spread throughout the lands bordering the Mediterranean. When Jews came from the outlying countries to Jerusalem the money they would bring was ordinarily the currency of their own lands. However, it was customary to pay a tax for the support of the Temple, and the tax was the local half-shekel. To assist the foreigners in paying this tax, money changers were in the Temple precincts who could change the foreign currency into the local currency. There was a small charge for this service, and the possibility of taking advantage of the unwary foreigner. Since foreign or pagan coins usually carried the image of a ruler, and thus violated the religious law forbidding graven images, they could not be used in the Temple. Money changing was thus a religious need as well as a convenience.

All this Temple commerce was under the control of the chief priestly families. They not only benefited financially from this

86

control but were able to become quite rich through the taxes, sales of animals, money changing, and the offerings reserved for them.

Temple sacrifice was prescribed by the Law of Moses for a number of ordinary events in family life. It was in submission to this prescription that Mary and Joseph went to the Temple after the birth of Jesus to offer what the Law required — a pair of turtle-doves or two pigeons. The birds were cut apart at the altar and burned on the bed of coals.

Observance of the Law

The rules for Temple worship and for much of Jewish life were spelled out in the Law. Over and over we hear references to the Law. What was it, and where did it come from? The Law, or the Torah, was made up of the first five books of the Bible: Genesis, Exodus, Leviticus, Numbers, and Deuteronomy. These books describe the origins of the world and the Jewish people, their Covenant with God, and the way this Covenant was to be observed. Jewish religion, Jewish commerce, Jewish political life, and Jewish daily life were regulated by the prescriptions in the Law.

A good man was a man who lived according to the Law. A sinner was one who did not observe the Law. When people were referred to as religiously observant or nonobservant what they were observing or not observing was the Law.

In addition to the five books included in the Law, religious teachers had developed an entire body of interpretations of the Law. And there were interpretations of the interpretations. These

Another view of Avi-Yonah's model, showing the Temple itself

subsequent additions to the law were also considered to be part of the Law and to be binding. The original Law, the first five books of the Bible, were straightforward and clear compared with the subsequent interpretations of them. The people referred to by Jesus as the lawyers, or teachers of the Law, or scribes were schooled in the complexities of the Law and, especially, in the complex interpretations that had developed. They frequently used their knowledge, which only they possessed and which was necessary for correct legal observance, as a tool to manipulate people. And Jesus also accused them of making their own interpretations to be more important than the Law and of actually perverting the intention of the Law.

From the time of Kings David and Solomon to the time of Christ the role of Jerusalem and its Temple in the life of the country had grown so that, during the life of Christ, Jerusalem held an unparalleled place. When King David was extending his rule over the land he and the religious leaders equated worship in Jerusalem with orthodox worship. The people of Israel had been accustomed to worship in different shrines and temples, and the older books of the Bible record the existence of altars at different locations. One by one these places were destroyed, until only the Temple in Jerusalem remained. The kings and priests were able to impress on the country the belief that true worship could take place only in Jerusalem and that sacrifices made in other places, such as the renegade temple in Alexandria, were idolatrous, unacceptable to God, and disloyal. By the time of Jesus the place of Jerusalem in the religious life of the country had long been established. For this reason Jesus told his followers that the Messiah had to go to Jerusalem and could die only in Jerusalem.

7
THE SYNAGOGUE

"He came to Nazara, where he had been brought up, and went into the synagogue on the sabbath day as he usually did . . . " (Luke 4:16).

Today the word synagogue is common in our vocabulary, and the place itself a familiar sight in our communities. During the life of Jesus the synagogue had just become a commonly accepted place, for it was a relatively new institution. It represented a development in Jewish religion and Jewish culture. It was a result of the Hellenization of Jewish culture. The development of the synagogue gives us a first-rate summary of Jewish history in the years just before the time of Christ.

The Synagogue

The word *synagogue* comes from a Greek word that refers to community. It is no accident that it is a Greek word, for synagogues were one of the chief products of the Hellenization we described earlier. The religious ideal among the Jews, as we just noted, was to worship in the Temple in Jerusalem. Not only was it the ideal but other places were suspect. But with the dispersion of the Jewish people throughout the Mediterranean world, a dispersion brought about in part because of the better opportunities in the empire's bigger cities and in part by persecution, the ideal of worship in Jerusalem was no longer realistic. For many people Jerusalem was too far away for frequent worship. Yet, the idea of sacrifice anywhere but in Jerusalem smacked of idolatry. The religious renewals and revivals over the centuries had involved reemphasizing the Temple and closing down the local shrines, since the local shrines and temples usually mixed the worship of local, pagan gods with the worship of the God of Israel. As a result, the Jewish people living outside the Holy Land had little opportunity to practice their faith in the way that was customary among Jews living near Jerusalem. So they developed their own ways, ways that were more compatible with life in a world far from Jerusalem and dominated by Greek culture.

Community Centers

The first synagogues were developed in Egypt among the Greek-speaking Jews. They were community centers where community affairs could be discussed, the education of the young assured, and simple, nonsacrificial worship could take place. The growth of the synagogue was given a major support by a series of political events involving Julius Caesar and Antipater, the father of King Herod, and the Jewish community in Egypt.

Recall, as we detailed earlier, that Julius Caesar went to Egypt to put down a revolt against Roman authority. More powerful than he had anticipated, the Egyptian forces trapped Caesar in Alexandria. When news of Caesar's plight reached Antipater in Judaea, Antipater dispatched troops to relieve Caesar. Antipater himself persuaded the large Jewish community in Alexandria to support Caesar, which they did. This support turned the situation in Caesar's favor.

Caesar never forgot the support he received from Antipater and the Jewish community. In gratitude, Caesar gave the Jews the right to maintain community centers for their affairs and worship, a privilege the Romans usually did not give to subject peoples. This official support, along with the need for some means to come together for communal and religious gatherings, gave the synagogue a legitimacy that spurred its growth.

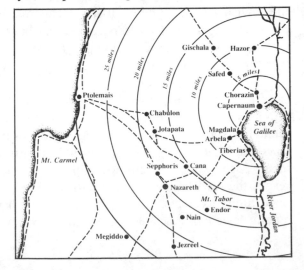

Capernaum and its environs

The synagogue at Capernaum. The ruins pictured here date from the early Third Century A.D. However, a 1954 excavation uncovered first-century foundations. At one end stood the ark or chest of the Law and in the center the lectern from which the Scriptures were read. The worshipers sat along the walls — the men downstairs, the women upstairs.

The religiously liberal Hellenistic culture contributed to the acceptance of the synagogue. From their initial appearance in Egypt they became common in other Greek-influenced regions and then in the Holy Land itself. The liberalizing tendency of Greek culture was paralleled by a democratizing movement within Judaism itself. This movement was led by groups of lay reformers, like the Pharisees, who were trying to wrest religious and political control of Jewish life from the hands of the aristocratic and chief priestly families, who had become very rich, powerful, and corrupt. Synagogue worship, unlike the Temple, did not need priests since it did not involve sacrifice. The Sabbath worship in the synagogue was nonsacrificial, but it was genuine worship and real prayer. Should there be priests and levites present during the synagogue worship they would be given a place of honor or asked to do the readings. But if none were present the service could proceed nonetheless.

Synagogue Worship

What was synagogue worship like? There are descriptions surviving which give us a picture of it. It was similar to Sabbath worship today in Jewish synagogues, with some of the inevitable changes that time and culture make. Synagogue worship, then as today, required ten men. It began with the common chanting of a prayer that is, today, the central part of the Sabbath service, the Shema Yisrael: "Hear, oh Israel, the Lord our God, the Lord is

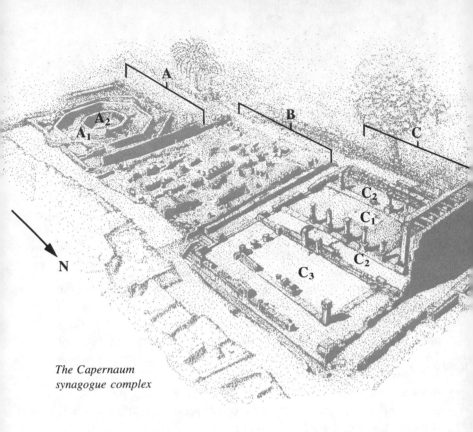

*The Capernaum
synagogue complex*

A St. Peter's house	B Residential area
A₁ Fifth-century octagonal church	C Synagogue
	C₁ Nave
A₂ Central room, where Jesus may have lived	C₂ Aisle
	C₃ Courtyard

One.'' This constant reaffirmation of Jewish monotheism, followed by the reminder not to worship any other gods, helps us understand why the Jewish people did not fit easily into the religion of the Greek and Roman world, with their dozens of gods and offhanded attitude toward worship.

In the synagogue, just as there is today, there was a chest or ark in which the scrolls of the Law were kept. After the Shema was chanted one of the men would stand before the ark and proclaim a series of praises, to which the people responded ''Amen.'' Then,

Ruins of the octagonal church

Another view of a corner of the octagonal church, with the Sea of Galilee in the background

one of the men took the scroll from the ark and brought it to the reading stand. Readers appointed from the congregation then read the appointed passages. The passages were established in a set cycle, much as there are regularly appointed readings in Catholic liturgy today. The reading was in Hebrew. The Hebrew in which the texts were written, an ancient Hebrew, was no longer a common language in everyday use. So there would be people at the synagogue service who would not understand the reading. To assist them there was a translator to translate into the common language. In the country where Jesus lived, in Galilee, this was Aramaic.

On certain days there was also a reading from the prophets. If there was someone present who was learned in the meaning of the texts, and usually this would be a scribe, he could give an explanation of the text. We are given an example of an explanation of the text in Saint Luke, in the continuation of the passage quoted at the opening of this section.

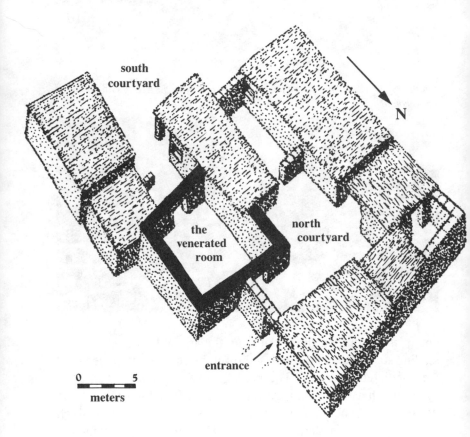

An artist's reconstruction of St. Peter's house. The large room, delineated in black, later became the central hall of the house/church. Why did this happen? Archaeologists state that perhaps as early as the middle of the First Century A.D. the floor, walls, and ceiling of this room were plastered. This was unusual in ancient Capernaum. The pottery used in the room also changed at this time. Before this period the pottery was like that found in other houses, designed for domestic use — cooking pots, bowls, etc. Once the room was plastered only storage jars and the remains of some oil lamps are found. For these and other reasons, some scholars believe that this was Jesus' Capernaum home.

"He came to Nazara, where he had been brought up, and went into the synagogue on the sabbath day as he usually did. He stood up to read, and they handed him the scroll of the prophet Isaiah. Unrolling the scroll he found the place where it is written:

The spirit of the Lord has been given to me,
for he has anointed me.
He has sent me to bring the good news to the poor,
to proclaim liberty to captives
and to the blind new sight,
to set the downtrodden free,
to proclaim the Lord's year of favour.

He then rolled up the scroll, gave it back to the assistant and sat down. And all eyes in the synagogue were fixed on him. Then he began to speak to them, 'This text is being fulfilled today even as you listen' '' (Luke 4:16-22).

From this passage we can see that there was a synagogue in Nazareth; that Jesus was authorized by the synagogue director to read; that he could read the Hebrew text; that he knew Isaiah well enough to edit the text; that there was an exposition of the text as part of the synagogue service. The verse preceding the quoted passage says: "Jesus . . . returned to Galilee . . . He taught in their synagogues . . . '' (Luke 4:14-15). So we know that there were a number of synagogues in Galilee. In fact, Galilee was one of the areas in which the development of the synagogue reached its high point.

The Spread of Christianity

Synagogues were not only significant to the Jewish community; they became a major influence in the spread of the Gospel. It was usually in the synagogues of the Greco-Roman world that the first Christian missionaries told of the death and Resurrection of Jesus. So the first Christian communities formed around the synagogue.

8
THE SCRIBES AND THE PHARISEES

"He had just finished speaking when a Pharisee invited him to dine at his house. He went in and sat down at the table. The Pharisee saw this and was surprised that he had not first washed before the meal. But the Lord said to him, 'Oh, you Pharisees! You clean the outside of cup and plate, while inside yourselves you are filled with extortion and wickedness . . . Alas for you lawyers also,' he replied 'because you load on men burdens that are unendurable, burdens that you yourselves do not move a finger to lift . . . Alas for you lawyers who have taken away the key of knowledge! You have not gone in yourselves, and have prevented others going in who wanted to' " (Luke 11:37-39,46,52).

Few groups loom as large in the New Testament as the scribes and the Pharisees. Frequently, they are mentioned together. This is why we group them together in this section. However, they were separate and distinct. Each group had its own purpose, history, and life. Occasionally, their membership overlapped. Mention is made at one point of the scribes of the Pharisees, indicating that there were scribes among the Pharisees. Some Pharisees may have studied to become scribes. And it is possible that some scribes, after the completion of their course of studies, may have joined the company of the Pharisees. But basically they were distinct groups.

The Pharisees

The Pharisees were members of a group known for living a strict and rigorous interpretation of the Jewish religious laws. The scribes were religious scholars, men who had become learned in the most important area of religious study, the interpretation of the Law. Each of these groups was held in high esteem by the people.

The name Pharisee means the "set apart." The implication was that they were set apart or separate because of their holiness. Thus, the name could also be understood to mean the holy ones. Were the Pharisees truly set apart? Yes, definitely. It is in this separation from the people that we find the essence of Pharisaism. The Pharisees were something like a religious order. They formed their own communities. They had their own application and entrance methods and definite, rigorous training procedures for their initiates, as in religious orders today.

The origins of the Pharisees go back before the time of Christ. The Book of Maccabees in the Old Testament recounts events about one hundred sixty years before the birth of Jesus. The Seleucid conqueror, Antiochus IV, determined to use force to Hellenize the Holy Land. In Jerusalem in the year 167 B.C. he massacred resisters, abolished Jewish practices, and turned the Temple into a Greek temple dedicated to Zeus. A priest named Mattathias, a grandson of Simeon the Hasmonean, started a revolt. Mattathias' son, Judas Maccabaeus, continued the revolt and finally defeated the Seleucids. Judas Maccabaeus established a powerful, independent Jewish kingdom. His family, known as the Hasmoneans, became the new royal family.

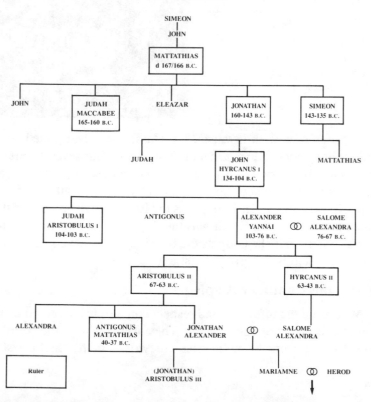

THE HASMONEANS

The Essenes' monastery at Qumran on the shores of the Dead Sea. Excavations have revealed a writing room (with dried ink in some of the inkwells), baths for ritual washings, and a kitchen. Occupation of the site ended with the Roman invasion, at which time the scroll library was hidden in nearby caves.

Cave Four, near Wadi Qumran, where fragments of over 300 books, biblical and nonbiblical, were discovered in 1952.

A group of Jewish loyalists, the Hassideans, had joined Mattathias and Judas Maccabaeus in their revolt. But several generations later, maintaining that the Hasmonean descendants of Judas had become soft and corrupt, the Hassideans broke with them and formed two groups. One group was the Essenes, who produced the Dead Sea Scrolls. The other was the Pharisees. By the time of the events recorded in the Gospels the Pharisees were a well-respected and well-established group in Israel.

From the Common People

Where did the influence and respect come from? To begin with, the Pharisees were commoners. They were men of the people. They did not come from the aristocracy or from the chief priestly families. In addition, they tried to extend Jewish religious practices to the ordinary people, an attempt looked on with favor by the people. Up until this attempt by the Pharisees many religious practices — mostly laws of purity concerning ritual washings, contact with foreigners, and contamination by other people and things considered unclean — were considered to apply only to the priests in the Temple. The prescriptions of the Law about ritual purity and many other legal requirements were not looked on as binding the people in the way they bound the religious elite. With the approach developed by the Pharisees, the ordinary people were allowed to have a role in the piety traditional to Judaism.

With this kind of support from the Pharisees the people did not need to see themselves as religiously second-class citizens. The fact that this piety was rather oppressive and that it was concerned with externals and not with inner dispositions, as Jesus noted in his criticisms of it, does not change the fact that, good or bad, it gave the people a share in religious practices that in previous centuries had not been open to them. They appreciated the change. Incidentally, Jesus does not criticize this extension of the piety to the people. In fact, he pushes it even further, requiring that interior dispositions match the external actions.

Because the Pharisees were primarily lay people and common people, they represented a major social movement. Israel had been a theocracy run by the hereditary priesthood and hereditary royalty. The Pharisees represented a new political force coming up out of the ranks of ordinary people. Religiously, they represented a force for the common people. The people held them in respect because they were advocates of the people. The Pharisees' background and theoretically democratic teachings on religion set them apart from the royalty and high priestly aristocracy.

Religious Communities

The Pharisees, as noted above, formed their own communities. They were family men and maintained their own homes, but they came together for study and worship and apparently maintained their own synagogues. The religious heart of the community was the agreement to observe the ritual laws on purity. New members underwent a period of trial, somewhat like a novitiate, during which time they were expected to observe all these laws very strictly. After successfully completing the period of trial, which could run from several months to a year or two, they were initiated into the community. Ordinarily, they were received into the community by the Pharisees' scribes. By law, scribes had the legal right to receive oaths and vows.

A Pharisee wearing phylacteries. These are small black leather boxes, containing parts of the Scriptures, which are fastened to the forehead and arm during recital of morning prayers.

Because the Pharisees spent a considerable amount of time and energy both on observing and interpreting the laws of ritual purity they developed their own school of legal interpretation. Their teachings regulated not only what one ate but the ritual washings of dishes and cooking utensils, physical contact with people and places considered unclean, personal washings before eating or after coming from the market, etc. Because of the Pharisees' public standing and the seriousness with which they observed these laws their interpretations became a norm for everyone else, including the chief priests. The higher priests resented the Pharisees as common-born, religious newcomers, but were powerless to do anything about the Pharisees' standing. Historians record that on at least one occasion the high priest, who held his position by reason of family rank, not learning or training, had to go to the Pharisees' scribes to be instructed on exactly what to do and what to avoid in presiding at the Passover rite in the Temple. It is easy to imagine how galling this must have been for the aristocratic high priest.

The support given the Pharisees by the people was less than complete, however, because the Pharisees looked on the average man with somewhat the same contempt he received from the aristocrats and the priests. The Pharisees drew clear lines between themselves and the average people, who were unable to observe all the laws. They judged the people harshly for their lack of legal observance. However, the Pharisees came from the same background as the people, and the people were prepared to forgive them their haughtiness. They saw the Pharisees as examples of the way things ought to be, even though they, the people, were unable to be that strict and observant.

The Scribes

Alongside the Pharisees is the group we know as the scribes. Who were they, and why was their influence so great? To answer these questions we need to know what it meant to become a scribe. The scribes were men who had learned the Law and its interpretations through a very demanding program of study. They were religious scholars, the theologians of their day. They were also ordained. They were not ordained in the way that the priests were set aside for their service in the Temple nor in the way that Catholic priests are ordained today. Rather, it would be more like the ordination that takes place in those churches in the Protestant tradition that do not believe in a separate priesthood. It was a public recognition given to specially trained and educated men. So these two elements were necessary before a man could be accepted into the group known as scribes. He needed considerable education and learning about the Law, its interpretation, and its application. And he had to be ordained.

Scribes were men of influence because they lived in a country where nothing was more important than knowing how to apply the Law accurately. The Jewish people were religious; religion was made concrete through living according to the Law; the Law was complex and needed expert interpretation, so to live religiously required experts to tell you how to do it.

Interpreting the Law

In the Holy Land in the time of Christ the religious laws did not cover only those things we would associate with religion. In a world in which everything comes from God and is referred back to God, and that was the Jewish view, everyday commerce had its religious dimension. In addition to the matters of ritual purity mentioned earlier, the religious laws covered such matters as inheritance, eligibility for marriage, keeping and breaking contracts and business agreements, betrothals and marriage contracts, questions of divorce, buying and selling goods and property, the validity of oaths, and questions of liability in cases of injury and wrong. With the specialized knowledge that told them how all these matters were to be arranged the scribes became men of great power. They could interpret the Law, and they could interpret and extend the whole body of tradition that came from the Law. They were deferred to, they were given the title of Rabbi, and they were held in respect.

Their influence went beyond simple matters of religion. Through their learning and because they were able to outshine all others in the holiness of their decisions, they effectively became the court of last resort in religious matters. Their influence extended even to worship in the Temple. With the development of many legal fine points it had become increasingly more difficult to meet the requirements of the Law regarding worship in the Temple. The difficulty stemmed from the increasing buildup of interpretations about the Law, and these interpretations had to be observed. Additionally, the presence of Greek and Roman armies of occupation, whose very presence in the Temple precincts could defile the Temple and require new acts of purification, made questions of purification very important. Knowing how to interpret the tradition concerning worship and concerning ritual purity became a matter of importance, even for the most highly placed priestly families. As much as they wanted to, the chief priests could no longer ignore the opinion of the scribes because everyone recognized that the scribes knew more religious law than any others. As a result of their learning the scribes began to work their way into positions of influence and importance. They were given the judicial positions in the local synagogues, and they even gained seats in the Sanhedrin.

Scholars who have studied contemporary records point out that many of the scribes came from humble origins. We can assume that the aristocracy and the upper classes were not pleased to see men from poor and plebian families moving into the positions that, heretofore, they themselves had held. The history of the scribes, like that of the Pharisees, is the story of major social change. Like it or not, the religious and lay aristocrats had little choice but to go along with the situation; for the scribes, through their learning, had made themselves an indispensable force in the life of the land. The people were religious, at least to the extent that they required that the public religious traditions be observed. The scribes were the only ones who could explain how this was to be done. As a result they developed a strong grasp on much of the life of the country, and they used that grasp to advance their own position.

Secret Knowledge

Today's prophets-teachers (Roberts, Hagin, et al)

The learning which the scribes possessed included a body of knowledge which was transmitted orally and which was not written down anywhere. The scribes, and only the scribes, were privy to this important oral tradition, some of which was mystical and some of which concerned interpretation of the Law. But all together it formed a body of esoteric knowledge to which only the initiate had access. In many ways this esoteric knowledge was the trump card held by the scribes. Like the prophets of old, they appeared to know things other people did not know. They could comment on the Law and speak about God in a way that went beyond the learning of other men, even though these men might be members of the chief priestly families. They had a special knowledge, a secret knowledge, and only they had it. This placed them in a position of considerable influence, an influence that went beyond simple political or military power. Because of this knowledge they received the veneration given to holy men in a culture where holy men are venerated. They were holy not by the virtue of their lives but because they were in contact with what was holy: the special and secret knowledge of God revealed to the prophets and transmitted orally to their most recent heirs, the scribes.

"Woe to you, scribes and Pharisees!"

Jesus criticizes the Pharisees and the scribes very severely. The reasons for this criticism are summed up in the passage quoted at the beginning of this section. The Pharisees separated exterior actions from interior dispositions. They were concerned with what men saw. And in so doing they ignored what was more important, the interior dispositions. The scribes were unwilling to share their knowledge openly and freely. They were the heirs of an important tradition, but they used their heritage for their own political and social benefit. For this reason Jesus accuses them of having "taken away the key of knowledge" (Luke 11:52).

9
THE PRIESTS AND THE LEVITES

"In the days of King Herod of Judaea there lived a priest called Zechariah who belonged to the Abijah section of the priesthood . . . Now it was the turn of Zechariah's section to serve, and he was exercising his priestly office before God when it fell to him by lot, as the ritual custom was, to enter the Lord's sanctuary and burn incense there. And at the hour of incense the whole congregation was outside, praying" (Luke 1:5,8-10).

During the life of Jesus the Holy Land was on the edge of being a theocracy, a land run by religious leaders according to religious rules. It was not a theocracy, because the religious leaders had to share their power with the Herods and with the governors appointed by Rome. But the religious leaders and religious law affected the day-to-day life of the people.

The Priests

At the top of the ladder of religious leaders were the priests. Historical developments had separated the priests into different social classes, so not all of them were as highly placed as others. At the top was a powerful aristocracy, and the aristocrats treated the rest of the priests very badly. The majority, in turn, resented the aristocrats very much.

All priests were from within the tribe of Levi and descended from Aaron, the brother of Moses. The priesthood was hereditary, and priestly families kept strict records of their descent in order to record their right to serve. One priestly family stood out above the others. This was the family of Zadoq. Zadoq was the high priest during the reign of King David and his son Solomon, when the Temple was built in Jerusalem. Because it was associated with this magnificent religious edifice, the Temple priesthood gained a further note of specialness. The family of Zadoq maintained that they had been high priests since the time of Aaron himself. The popular history agreed. They served as high priests until two

104

Cairo, Elephantine, Qumran

hundred years before the birth of Christ. Placing the time of Moses and Aaron at 1230 B.C., we can assign the family of Zadoq a continuity of over one thousand years. This priestly continuity was important to the people of Israel.

Then, around 175 B.C., something terrible happened. The Seleucid ruler, Antiochus IV, tried to impose his own Greek culture on the land and the people. He deposed the Zadoqite high priest and replaced him with a priest of his own choice, a priest who had paid Antiochus handsomely for the office. Because of the public outcry the new high priest did not last long, but the damage had been done. The chain of legitimate descent had been broken. Turmoil resulted. Several years passed when there was no high priest at all.

Coin of Antiochus IV. In his attempt to Hellenize the Jews, he had a pig sacrificed on the altar in Jerusalem, and destroyed all the books of Scripture he could find.

A generation later the descendants of Judas Maccabaeus, the national hero whose family of Hasmoneans ruled the country, also took on the high priesthood. They held it until the time of Herod. The last of them, a young man named Aristobulus who was the brother of King Herod's Hasmonean queen, Mariamne, had the misfortune to be competent, good-looking, and popular with the people. To the paranoid Herod, he looked like a possible rival. So on one hot afternoon Herod induced the youth to join Herod's guards in the swimming pool in the Jericho palace. In the guise of horseplay, the guards, acting under instructions from Herod, held the young man's head under the water until he drowned. From then on, Herod saw to it that no one would be high priest for more than a few years just so that there could be no public rival to his own power.

From the time that Herod began appointing his high priests until the public ministry of Jesus is a period of about seventy years. There were about twenty high priests during this time. What is remarkable is that they all came from three or four families. They were families that used power, influence, and money to get the

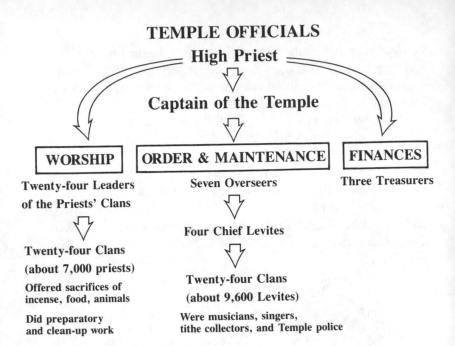

TEMPLE OFFICIALS

High Priest

Captain of the Temple

WORSHIP	ORDER & MAINTENANCE	FINANCES
Twenty-four Leaders of the Priests' Clans	**Seven Overseers**	**Three Treasurers**
	Four Chief Levites	
Twenty-four Clans (about 7,000 priests)	**Twenty-four Clans (about 9,600 Levites)**	
Offered sacrifices of incense, food, animals	Were musicians, singers, tithe collectors, and Temple police	
Did preparatory and clean-up work		

high priesthood. Once they had control of the priesthood they tried to keep it in the family. And they succeeded. They were cruel, arrogant, and greedy. They took all the positions of importance in the Temple in Jerusalem, kept control of the Temple's revenues, had their bands of bullies to take care of anyone who protested, and cared little that the people saw them as hypocrites. Their agents also stole from the common priests the pittance that came to them for their work in the Temple. The high priestly families' religious illegitimacy increased the hatred and resentment shown them by the people.

Work of the High Priest

What was the actual work of the priesthood? We will describe their work, beginning with the high priest. Once a year, on the Day of Atonement, he entered the Holy of Holies and sprinkled the blood of a sacrificed bull seven times. As we would expect, there were very detailed rituals he had to perform that day before daring to enter the Holy of Holies. The high priest was also privileged to take part in any sacrifice in the Temple whenever he wanted. Many of the animals that were offered in the Temple were given in part to the priests, and the high priest had first choice of what he wanted.

High priest clothed in the vestment called the ephod. Attached to the ephod was a breastplate with twelve precious stones, representing the twelve tribes of Israel.

In addition to presiding on the Day of Atonement, the high priest was required by religious law to perform or pay for several other ceremonies and sacrifices during the year. One restriction placed on the high priest was in his choice of a wife. He had to marry a virgin of pure Israelite descent.

The high priest was also the head, ex officio, of the Sanhedrin. The Sanhedrin was a council of priests and elders. It had the responsibility for administering the country's affairs within the limits imposed by Roman authority. Its authority and jurisdiction had varied considerably over the years. At one point, several generations before the birth of Christ, it was the council for Jerusalem, and other cities had their respective councils. During the life of Christ, it was the only council in the kingdom. It had seventy-one members drawn from the chief priestly families, the aristocracy, and the scribes. It was a religious supreme court with jurisdiction in both civil and criminal cases.

Before the birth of Christ, its authority was nominal at best. It had made the mistake of accusing the young Herod of cruelty, and many of its members sided with the Hasmonean prince, Antigonus, who was put on the throne by the Parthians in their attempt to seize the country in 40 B.C. When Herod returned as king in 37 B.C. he executed the majority of the members, replacing them with his own men. During the years of Jesus' ministry the Sanhedrin was more powerful, and was presided over by the high priest. Because of its function as a religious court the presence of scribes became more and more necessary.

Captain of the Temple

Next on the list of religious leaders, below the high priest, was the captain of the Temple. The captain was a combination of general manager and police chief. If we see the high priest as responsible for the worship in the Temple, then the captain was responsible for everything else. To grasp the size of his responsibility, we should recall that daily life in the Temple involved thousands and thousands of visitors and pilgrims; employees numbering in the hundreds, except when major repairs would increase this into the thousands; public and private sacrifices every day; plus the repair and maintenance of the Temple. The captain had his own police force, and it was this police force that came to arrest Jesus after he was betrayed. During the time of Jesus, the captain of the Temple was a member of the high priestly aristocracy and frequently became high priest himself. If the high priest should be prevented from functioning on the Day of Atonement, as happened from time to time because of some ritual impurity, the captain of the Temple took his place. The captain of the Temple, like all the other men who served in any priestly function, had to be a member of a priestly family.

Functioning under the captain of the Temple were three groups. The first was composed of the leaders of the priests who directed the weekly and daily worship. Then there were Temple overseers who kept the keys to the Temple and saw to its security. Finally, there were three treasurers. In the hierarchy of importance, the priests in their religious function would have outranked the overseers and treasurers. But the overseers and treasurers lived in Jerusalem and were permanently employed in the Temple. The priests ordinarily lived in towns throughout the country and came to Jerusalem only for the weeks when they served, so their influence would have been less.

Duties of the Priests

Scholars estimate that during the life of Christ there were about seven thousand priests in Israel. They were divided into twenty-four tribes or clans. One by one, in rotation, the clans came to Jerusalem for a week to perform the services in the Temple. The services were divided into weekly, or Sabbath, services and the daily worship. Each clan had its leaders for the weekly and daily services. It was these leaders who formed the group that ranked with the overseers and treasurers in the Temple.

Each morning there was an offering of incense. Each morning a lamb was sacrificed and burned on the altar. Food was offered, as

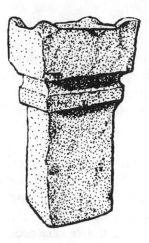

Stone horned altar found at Megiddo. The Tent of Meeting and the Jewish Temples contained two altars, one for incense and one for immolating animals. This one was for incense.

well as a special loaf of bread, either by the high priest or in his name. There was also a drink offering. These same services were repeated in the evening. For some of these offerings the presiding priests were chosen by lot.

Each morning the altar of holocausts had to be cleaned off, and each evening wood had to be brought in for the next day's sacrifices. All the acts of worship were performed according to a ritual. Each act of worship required its proper utensils or dishes. The priests were assigned different functions in the elaborate rituals.

On the Sabbath, in addition to these offerings, two lambs would be sacrificed. Twelve loaves of bread, representing the twelve original tribes, would be renewed. The number of priests involved in the morning and evening worship came to about three hundred men.

Historians record that when each of the twenty-four clans came to Jerusalem to take its turn serving in the Temple the villagers often came along with the priests. There is the impression that this week was a very special time; and the priests, their families, and their neighbors felt very privileged to be a part of it.

By law, only priests could enter the more important parts of the Temple. Because of this law, priests had to be trained in all the crafts necessary to repair and maintain the Temple. If this law also applied to charwomen, then priests were needed for the ordinary cleaning of the Temple. In this age before machines, when all heavy work had to be done by the muscles of men and animals, there had to be a large number of priests for any heavy work.

The priests came from their towns to Jerusalem twice each year to perform their week-long service. In addition, they came for each of the three festivals that attracted pilgrims to Jerusalem — Passover, Pentecost, and the Feast of Tabernacles. During these festival times, some of the ordinary priests had some responsibilities in the Temple.

Most of the priests were poor. According to the old Law, they should have been supported by tithes and other taxes, but most people did not pay them. There was an enormous gap separating the average priest from the chief priestly families. The average priests survived through their own hard labors, and, like most poor people at the time, they did not survive all that well. When they performed their services in the Temple in Jerusalem they were entitled to receive certain offerings, such as the animal hides from the sacrifice victims, as their day's pay. Historians report that the high priest's Temple police usually took them from the ordinary priests, frequently by force. It is no surprise, then, that the animosities between the ordinary priests and the members of the priestly aristocracy ran deep.

The Levites

At the bottom of the ladder of those providing religious services in the Temple were the Levites. Who were they, and how were they different from the priests? As in all matters concerning Temple worship, the answer is based on family descent. The Levites were members of the tribe of Levi. They were descendants of another group of priests who, in ancient times, served in the religious shrines that existed throughout the land. However, the Levites were not descended from Aaron, and thus did not qualify as true priests as the priesthood had come to be defined. As part of the religious development that led to the building of the Temple in Jerusalem, the countryside shrines known as high places were all shut down. The religion and worship in the high places had frequently mixed native religions and superstitions with Jewish worship and so were religiously suspect. The descendants of the priests who served in these shrines were known simply as Levites and were given minor functions in the Temple in Jerusalem. They provided the music for the worship and served as doorkeepers. Because they had the status of laity they were forbidden to enter the areas reserved to the priests. They sang, played instruments, and were given chores to do.

Like the priests, they were divided into twenty-four groups or clans and came to Jerusalem twice a year for their weekly service. At the top of the Levitic hierarchy were the musicians. They were at the top because the instrument players got closer to participating in the official Temple worship than any other laity. The Temple was divided into a series of courts, one beyond the other, increasing in holiness as they went toward the Holy of Holies. Right at the line that separated the court of the laity from the court of the priests was a platform reserved for the musicians. It was a few feet higher than the lay people's courtyard but a few feet lower than the priests' courtyard. This platform symbolizes the status of the Levites. However, the musicians who used this platform were considered to be specially honored and were required to prove that they truly descended from Levitic families.

The Levites were as poor as the regular priests. Some historians record that they were jealous of the privileges of the regular priests, even though the priests were no better off than they. Although the Levites were at the very bottom of the ladder of Temple officials, they were still above the average Jew. The average man was excluded from participation in the Temple, except on those days when he was offering a sacrifice, and he saw the worship of God as a privilege granted to a very special group of men. In the eyes of the average Israelite, the Levite was part of this group of special and privileged people. The Levite might be at the bottom of this religious ladder, but the ladder was one the average man would never even touch.

10
THE RELIGIOUS FESTIVALS

"It was the time when the feast of the Dedication was being celebrated in Jerusalem. It was winter, and Jesus was in the Temple walking up and down in the Portico of Solomon" (John 10:22-24).

"Just before the Jewish Passover Jesus went up to Jerusalem" (John 2:13).

"Some time after this there was a Jewish festival, and Jesus went up to Jerusalem" (John 5:1).

"As the Jewish feast of Tabernacles drew near, his brothers said to him, 'Why not leave this place and go to Judaea . . . ' Jesus answered ' . . . Go up to the festival yourselves: I am not going to this festival, because for me the time is not ripe yet' . . . However, after his brothers had left for the festival, he went up as well, but quite privately, without drawing attention to himself" (John 7:2-3,6,8-10).

Throughout the Gospels we hear references to the festivals celebrated by the Jewish people. There is the feast of Tabernacles, or of Booths, as it is translated in some Bibles. There is the Passover itself. There is the feast of Dedication. And in the above passages quoted from Saint John, Jesus goes to Jerusalem to celebrate each of these feasts. We know that they were important in the life of the nation, and they were obviously important to Jesus and his followers. But what were these feasts? Why were they so important, what were they about, and how were they celebrated?

Feasts of Remembering

Each of these feasts is still celebrated today in the Jewish community, and the reason for their celebration is much the same as it was in the time of Christ. The fact that the Jewish people would have maintained these feasts over the centuries says much about the importance of remembering. Remembering is a key to understanding these Jewish festivals and Jewish religion. Jewish children were taught to remember. More than anything else they

so, too, with Lord's Supper

were taught to remember. Remember who you are, remember what God has done for you and for us, and live as though you remember. And as we have seen, memory was the key to their learning. They were taught by having to remember everything.

The Jewish festivals were festivals of remembering. Either they were festivals of remembering what God had done for them, or remembering what he had ordered them to do, or remembering the days in their history when they had fallen from grace and had been restored through God's mercy. They were festivals designed to make the people remember that God was God, that man was only man, and that man owed everything to God.

The Covenant

These festivals also emphasized the contractual side of Jewish religion. We speak of the Old Testament, and we speak of the Covenant. Because of the specifically religious use that has been given to these words we overlook their basic meaning. Put simply, they were contracts. Jewish religion was a contractual religion. You do this for me, and I will do this for you — a contract in its simplest form. The form of contract that was at the heart of Jewish religion was the kind of contract that existed in the Middle East between powerful monarchs and weaker, vassal states. It was a diplomatic treaty between unequals. The Jewish people had seen and experienced the contracts or treaties between powerful rulers, like the pharoahs in Egypt and the kings of Assyria on the one hand and the weak nations they had subjugated on the other. They modeled their religion on these treaties. They would honor God, they would have no God before him, and he, in turn, would be their God. They would live by the rules he gave them, and he, in turn, would protect them as he saw fit. These festivals were all part of their honoring that contract which they had taken on themselves.

Nature Feasts

These festivals were also tied in with nature. Planting and harvesting and seasons and moons were all a part of these festivals. The Jewish people used these natural cycles to remind them of their God, of his goodness to them, of their obligation to him, and, especially, that he was the source of all life. They used these

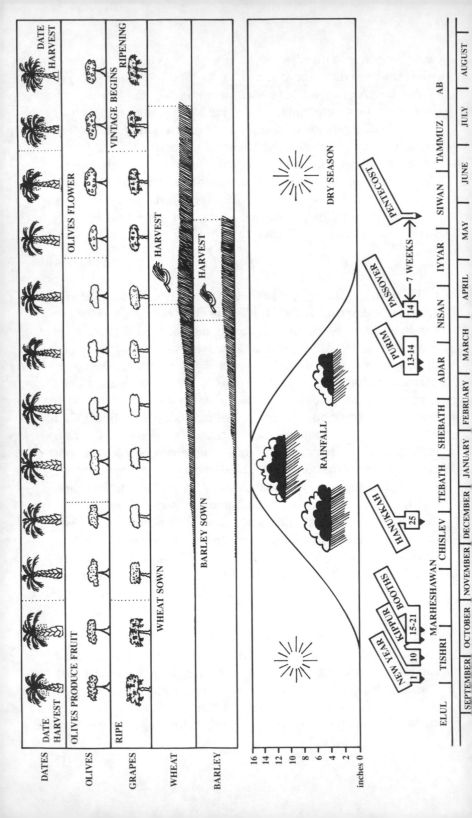

natural cycles to remind them of their God, but they also used them to remind themselves that he was One and that he was spirit.

What were these festivals? There were three important ones: Passover, Pentecost, and Tabernacles. In addition, there was the Dedication, which was more recent in origin. The New Year and Atonement celebrations, as we shall see, were part of the Tabernacles festival.

Passover

Passover recalled the events surrounding the Jewish people's flight from slavery in Egypt to freedom in the Promised Land. During the Passover time each family sacrificed a lamb, and in a very ritualized manner ate the lamb roasted, recalling the night when the angel of the Lord passed over the land of Egypt slaying the firstborn of every house, man and beast, except those houses marked with the blood of the lambs sacrificed at the command of Moses. Since the people fled during the night after their sacrificial meal, without time to allow the dough in their kneading bowls to rise, from that time on the days of Passover were called the Days of Unleavened Bread. At Passover, they ate only unleavened bread.

Jesus' Last Supper was his own celebration of the Passover with his apostles. In the Catholic Church today, the Holy Thursday celebration recalls the events of the Passover celebration in Jerusalem, and Christ's institution of the Eucharist at that supper. Because he would have used unleavened bread at that Last Supper, the Church today still uses unleavened bread in the Communion of the Mass.

In the Holy Land, people came to Jerusalem for the Passover if they could. The lambs that were eaten for Passover were all slaughtered by the priests in the Temple. This means that during the days of Passover Jerusalem and the Temple would have been beehives of activity, the streets full of pilgrims, the Temple full of fathers of families with their paschal lambs, and every place of accommodation filled to overflowing.

Pentecost

The second festival we will look into is called Pentecost. Christians know this day as one important to them, because it was on Pentecost that the Holy Spirit descended on the apostles. But that event took place on the Jewish feast of Pentecost, a celebration that goes back into the roots of Jewish history. It was known as the Feast of Weeks because it recalled the end of the barley harvest. The festival was to take place exactly seven weeks after the sickle was first applied to the ripening grain. The word Pentecost is no more than a Greek word referring to these fifty days.

Many generations before the time of Christ, Passover time, coming as it does with the first moon of spring, was established as the beginning of the grain harvest. Obviously, the harvest would vary from year to year, but for the sake of convenience the date was formalized. So Pentecost came exactly seven weeks after Passover. The days between Passover and Pentecost were known as the Days of Omer. *Omer* is the Hebrew word for sheaf, the bundle of harvested grain or straw that was brought to the threshing floor. So these Days of Omer were the days for bringing in the sheaves from the field to the threshing floor. At the end of the seven weeks two barley loaves, made from the new crop, were presented to the Lord in the Temple. This was a ceremonial way of ending the barley harvesting time and giving thanks for the harvest.

The celebration of Pentecost had an especially festive note to it, for the Days of Omer had been given a penitential character, somewhat like the Christian Lent. During this period, there were no weddings and no celebrations of note. These happy events took place after Pentecost, so we may imagine that the arrival of Pentecost was looked on as the beginning of a season of celebration. It would be a rare family that did not have a wedding taking place somewhere within the clan at Pentecost time.

The essence of the Pentecost celebration itself was a giving back to God what was his by creation and by right — life. This harvest celebration was an explicit recognition that life came from God, that the existence of the harvest and the crops was under the providence of God, and that it was no more than just for the people to give thanks for the harvest. They gave this thanks symbolically by offering two loaves of bread made from the harvested grain.

Feast of Tabernacles

The third festival is known as the Feast of Tabernacles. It is also referred to in some Bibles as the Feast of Tents or Booths. The difficulty with the translations comes from the fact that we do not use the structure referred to anymore, so we do not have an English word that describes it exactly.

The origins of the Feast of Tabernacles are both very Middle Eastern and also quite secular. The feast is another harvest festival based on two common practices. Summertime in the Holy Land is hot. At times, the heat can be almost unbearable. The sun heats up the very stones that the buildings are made of. Well into the night, even after the evening has begun to cool, the stone walls of the houses go on radiating heat.

In the time of Christ, the usual family house would be a series of small, low-roofed rooms centered around a larger, central room. It was quite common for married sons to live with their families in their parents' house. Each son would sleep with his family in one of the small rooms off the central room. As we can imagine, it would be common to have thirty or forty people living in one house, counting the parents, the children and daughters-in-law, and the children's children.

Imagine a large number of people trying to sleep in poorly ventilated, small, overcrowded quarters, the stone walls still radiating the day's heat. Breathing would be a problem, to say nothing of sleeping. There was only one, safe solution — to sleep on the roof in the cool air of the night under the stars. And this is what people did. Even today in the Arab villages it is common to see bedding set out on the roof of stone houses during the summer months.

However, most people like some sort of protection, some light shelter to keep the ghosts of night away. So they built, and still build, light structures over the sleeping areas, light enough to let the air pass through and the stars to shine through but solid enough to diminish the sense of being totally exposed. They built from sticks, from leaves, and from palm fronds.

At harvest time, when the summer crops and the fruit from the orchards would be ready for gathering, people would do the same in their fields. In the Holy Land, the farmers live in the villages and have their fields outside the villages. In their fields it was, and still is, common to build towers — round, stone structures eight or ten feet across and somewhat more from ground to top. The tower provided a place to stay during the harvest and to take shelter in if necessary. It served the other uses a farmer in our own country

A stone watchtower in a field. These observation posts served as a protection against thieves and wild animals.

might have for a barn or a shed. At harvest time, the farmer would go to his land outside the village and stay there, using the tower as a house. Here, too, he would follow the practice of sleeping on the roof of the tower, under the shelter of the booth or tabernacle built on top of it. Religious laws required that the structure be light enough for the stars to be seen through the roof.

Now, what makes this practice a religious one? Nothing. It is completely secular in its origin and purpose. What made it religious was the decision to use it religiously as a means of remembering the role of God in their lives. The Feast of Tabernacles was a fall festival, and it matched the spring harvest festival. They used this harvest practice, the construction of the booths, to remind themselves of God's goodness to them in giving them the land, the growth of their crops, and the harvest. To give the practice of building the booths a specifically religious connection, rules were laid down governing their construction.

The Feast of Tabernacles came at the end of a special period that included the New Year and the Day of Atonement. Tabernacles was the culmination of the period that included these three celebrations. To see the Feast of Tabernacles as separate from the other two days would be to lose sight of a unity that was important to the people. It would also underestimate the importance of New Year's and the Day of Atonement.

New Year's Day was a memorial. Originally, it was probably a commemoration of the dead. Many primitive people believed that the spirits of the dead came back to visit their living relatives at the beginning of the year. The Jewish feast was possibly influenced by this belief. But the prime theme of this Day of Remembrance or commemoration, as it was also described, was the fact of remembering itself. For the reasons given above, memory and remembering were religious acts in and of themselves.

Yom Kippur

New Year's came on the first of the month. On the tenth day of the month came the Atonement, what we know as Yom Kippur. Like the Passover, it was a solemn celebration. Its purpose was to purify the priests for their service in the Temple, the people from their faults, and the sanctuary itself so that it would be a fit place for worship. It was during this day's rites of purification that the high priest played so important a role. In addition to sprinkling the Holy of Holies with the blood of a sacrificial animal, which we described earlier, he was also involved in washings and in an incensing that could be seen as a fumigation.

The Temple rites took place out of sight and sound of most of the people. What was probably the most impressive rite for them was the practice of leading a goat from the sanctuary out into the wilderness. In a symbolic rite within the Temple, the sins of the people were laid on the goat. Then the goat was led off ''to Azazel.'' Azazel was a mythic spirit who lived in the wilderness, the wilderness where God never went. The goat was led out of the city on a special causeway, so constructed that no one would be able to reach the animal. Pagans living in Jerusalem sought to touch the goat so that their sins, too, could be laid on it and they would be freed from them. But the goat was only for the benefit of the Jewish people, not for the pagans. The goat was led in procession a dozen miles out of Jerusalem. For the last mile, the priest who was chosen to lead the goat walked with it alone and led it to a ravine. There the priest pushed it off the precipice to fall to its death below.

The word *kippur* does not mean atonement, it means a cleansing or a purgation. The atoning was accomplished by means of these purgations. Considering the fact that personal sinfulness and ritual impurity were so real a part of human life, this opportunity to be freed from sin was very important to people. We can imagine the sense of relief that would come to everyone, priests and people, when they heard that the rites they were bound to carry out had been accomplished successfully.

It was after this period of purgation, and at the end of the gathering of the crops, that the Feast of Tabernacles took place. Considering that it was preceded both by a purgation from sin and a successful harvest, we can understand the festive quality that Tabernacles had in the minds of the people.

Hanukkah

One other festival is mentioned in the Gospel, the Feast of Dedication. This was a relatively minor feast, of the more recent past, so it is not among those listed in the Scripture. It recalled the purification and rededication of the Temple in 164 B.C. When Antiochus IV turned the Temple into a pagan temple dedicated to Zeus it became, according to Jewish religious law, unfit for worship. After Judas Maccabaeus drove out the Seleucid Greek rulers and established his independent, Jewish kingdom, he had to have the Temple rededicated and purified before worship could be resumed. The Feast of Dedication recalled that event when in 164, three years to the day after Antiochus placed the statue of Zeus in the Temple, Judas reopened the Temple. This celebration was also known as Hanukkah and occurred in the winter. It was not as important as the three seasonal feasts: Passover, Pentecost, and Tabernacles.

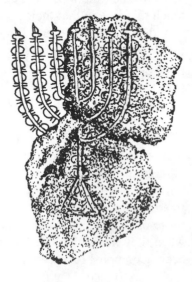

Plaster fragments of the earliest known representation of the Temple "menorah," from the reign of Herod, found in excavations in the Old City of Jerusalem.

PART FOUR:
SOCIAL
AND
ECONOMIC
BACKGROUND

11
SOCIAL CLASSES IN THE HOLY LAND

"A member of one of the leading families put this question to him, 'Good Master, what have I to do to inherit eternal life?' Jesus said to him, ' . . . You know the commandments . . . ' He replied, 'I have kept all these from my earliest days till now.' And when Jesus heard this he said, 'There is still one thing you lack. Sell all that you own and distribute the money to the poor . . . then come, follow me.' But when he heard this he was filled with sadness, for he was very rich" (Luke 18:18-23).

"There was a rich man who used to dress in purple and fine linen and feast magnificently every day. And at his gate there lay a poor man called Lazarus, covered with sores, who longed to fill himself with the scraps that fell from the rich man's table. Dogs even came and licked his sores" (Luke 16:19-21).

There were leading families in the Holy Land, and they were very rich. As these passages indicate, the rich could dress in purple and fine linen and feast magnificently every day. And there were poor people. The poor were left to die in the streets. This gives us a brief picture of the extremes in the land of Jesus. The records left by chroniclers and the buildings unearthed by archaeologists indicate that this picture is accurate. We also know that there were classes in between the extremes. To gain a fuller picture of the social classes in the Holy Land, we will describe them, beginning with the palaces in Jerusalem.

The Royal Court

At the very top of the social ladder was the royal court. The court reached its most luxurious and ostentatious stage during the reign of Herod the Great. Jewish law permitted the king to have many wives, and Herod had ten. By these wives he had a number of children. These children had royal rank, and when they reached adulthood would have been men and women of economic and political influence. Marriage was a way of cementing relation-

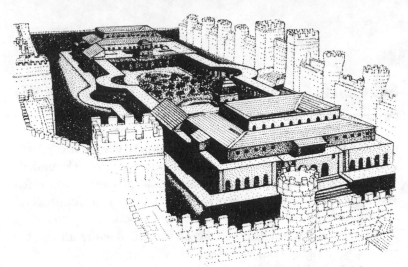

Herod the Great's palace, as represented in Avi-Yonah's model

ships with tribes and groups whose friendship the king was seeking, so the women's quarters in the palace were large.

King Herod had his officials and personal servants. His dependents had their own servants, slaves, manservants, and ladies-in-waiting. The palaces that Herod had in Jerusalem were large. His upper palace was about the same size as the central portion of the Temple; and his second palace, while smaller, was still a major building. The members of his household, and there were many of them, were housed in great luxury.

Jerusalem had become the capital city for a strategically important country in the Roman Empire. It was a religious capital for a group of people who had significant communities in the major cities in the empire. It was the administrative center for a kingdom that had become quite prosperous. As a result, there were civil and religious leaders with considerable wealth at their disposal. Spartan living was not seen as a virtue among the rich, and people who had money would have considered it quite normal to spend it on living well.

The austerity that we associate with the early Christian communities and with religious leaders like the Pharisees and the Essenes and John the Baptist was unheard of within these palace walls. Great banquets, receptions for visiting dignitaries, great public spectacles like those in the major Roman cities, and visible luxury were all part of court life.

The Wealthy Class

Like any capital city, Jerusalem had its wealthy people who were not members of the royalty. They were members of the chief priestly families, wealthy landowners, and rich merchants. The best land in the country was owned by the Romans, the members of Herod's family, or other rich and powerful people, most of whom maintained palaces in Jerusalem. For some of the rich, the source of their income was in Jerusalem itself. But it was common for the rich to live in Jerusalem, no matter what the source of their income, because Jerusalem had an active social life in which banquets and entertainments played a large part.

As is pointed out in the Gospel, there was a well-established protocol both in inviting guests and in seating them once they arrived. Guests expected that on the actual day of the banquet a personal invitation would be ceremonially delivered from the host as a way of paying respect to the status of the guest.

Our acquaintance with Jerusalem comes principally from the Gospels. We should keep in mind that Jesus and his followers came from somewhere else. We do not get an insider's view of Jerusalem in the Gospels. Further, most of the people we hear about in the Gospels are not the rich and the powerful. From the picture drawn for us, it would be possible to overlook the presence of a wealthy class and the fact that this class had the means to pay for a luxurious life.

The Middle Class

In Jerusalem, there was also a group analogous to our middle class. The three major pilgrimages made to Jerusalem each year created a religious tourist industry similar to the tourist industries we find today in pilgrimage centers like Rome and Lourdes. This pilgrimage industry helped to create a merchant class.

At the top of the merchant class were the men who bought and sold in bulk and stored their goods in warehouses. Archaeologists tell us that Jerusalem had many warehouses during the time of Herod the Great. Next would be the shop owners. There were no factories during this period, and all the manufactured goods came from small shops. The shop owners might be craftsmen with a business large enough to merit hiring a few other craftsmen to assist them, or they may have had only their family members helping them. There were skilled craftsmen and laborers who hired themselves out to the merchants and shop owners for a daily wage.

The goods made locally or imported in bulk and stored in warehouses before reaching the consumer were oriented principally toward supporting either the pilgrims or the Temple. The goods included the food consumed at the festival times, the gifts bought by pilgrims, and clothing worn at the celebrations. During the time of Jesus, the people spent money on these celebrations, and a significant portion was spent in Jerusalem, a practice favored by the religious customs. This practice of buying goods required for the celebrations in Jerusalem created a prosperity in the city as well as an extraordinary inflation in costs.

The Poor

In the midst of all this prosperity were the poor people. The Gospels refer to poor people, such as the woman who placed her two small coins in the Temple treasury. There is the prescription of the law which allows poor people to offer two doves in the place of the customary animal. Reference is made to freedmen; so there were both slaves and former slaves, and they were poor. The parable about the vineyard workers indicates that there were day laborers who were dependent on finding work each day, and they were poor. Some of the priests who were not connected with the chief priestly families were impoverished by the greed of these families.

How did the poor survive? In part, through their labors. In part, they survived through welfare. The welfare took different shapes. There were public works projects which helped the unemployed. Herod the Great undertook some of his major efforts, like street paving projects, apparently to cope with unemployment in Jerusalem. In addition, it was customary for pilgrims to give alms to the poor, and we may assume that the poor begged. However, as contemporary evidence indicates, the poor did not survive very well and, in times of severe hardship, not for very long.

The scribes, the Pharisees, and the other religious people like Jesus were numbered among the poor. Religious law did not allow teachers to receive money for their work. In this, they differed from the chief priests who were enriched through their work.

126

The knowledge of the wealthy class we gain through the Scriptures is limited because Jesus dealt infrequently with the rich. There was the rich young man who asked what he must do to be perfect. During the arrest and trial of Jesus we receive a description of the high priest's house, apparently a small palace, for it had a gatehouse, courtyard, and a meeting room large enough to house the entire Sanhedrin. Except for these and a few other incidents, Jesus worked mostly with the poor.

Outside Jerusalem

This gives us a picture of life in Jerusalem, but what of the rest of the country? What was life like in other cities and in the countryside? Do we have information that allows us to answer these questions? Yes, we do. We can come up with a picture of relative prosperity throughout the Holy Land during the life of Christ. We will give examples of this prosperity, going from the south to the north.

To the south of the Holy Land is the kingdom of the Nabataeans. While politically and culturally distinct from the Jewish kingdom, Nabataea was a close neighbor. Galilee, for example, was over twice as far from Jerusalem as the Nabataean border. Since Herod's mother was a Nabataean, there were family ties with the Nabataeans as well. The kingdom included the southern end of the Dead Sea, and its border was only fifty miles from Jerusalem.

Nabataea is a striking example of the prosperity to be found in the Near East. Through an extraordinary system of cisterns and irrigation it had turned the Negev Desert into a prosperous wine-producing region. Their cities were large and well-planned complexes of stone buildings with well-laid-out streets, large ware-

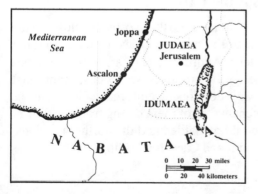

The kingdom of Nabataea, during Herod the Great's time

127

Herod's summer palace at Masada, about 3½ miles from the Dead Sea. Two aqueducts, cisterns, bath houses, workshops, barracks, and the palace itself have been excavated.

houses, impressive public buildings, and palaces for the rich. The cities provided both shelter and trading opportunities for the caravans going from Gaza on the coast and Egypt into Arabia and for traders traveling on the north-south route.

A few dozen miles north of the Nabataean border Herod had built fortresses on mountaintops overlooking the Dead Sea. One, Kypros, was named for his mother. The other was Masada, most famous for the siege that took place after the time of Christ. These fortresses provided protection for the traders on the north-south route, from Syria in the north to Arabia and Egypt in the south. Just below the fortified volcano peak that Herod named after his mother is the ancient city of Jericho. Herod built a palace there. From the ruins surrounding the remains of the palace, we can conclude that there were substantial farm communities and trading centers.

Prosperity throughout the Land

Throughout Judaea and Samaria, farther north and closer to the Mediterranean Sea, are the ruins of other cities founded or rebuilt by Herod and other rulers: Antipatris, Caesarea, Sebaste, Nicopolis. Throughout the land there are, even today, significant traces of a prosperous, well-developed, cultured society with its own aristocracy and merchants, all of them dating from the time of Christ. The same can be said of Galilee and the northern regions, where Tiberias, Capernaum, and Caesarea Philippi can be seen as examples of prosperity.

It is common for people to think of the Negev Desert and imagine a wilderness, to think of Galilee and imagine shepherds and poor fishermen, to think of Jerusalem and imagine narrow streets and twisted alleys. There was a wilderness to the east of the Jordan, but there was also real prosperity in the Negev. There were shepherds and poor fishermen in Galilee, but there were also stone houses, colonnaded streets, impressive public buildings, and warehouses for merchants. And by the time that Jesus entered upon his public ministry, there were very few narrow twisted streets left in Jerusalem. Herod had rebuilt the city along a Roman model, and he had created a magnificent capital of wide, paved streets running at right angles to each other at regular intervals, magnificent public buildings, and excellent facilities for the city's merchants. The Jerusalem we see today is a medieval city, very different from the city Jesus knew.

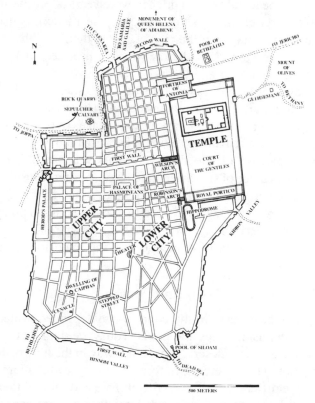

The city of Jerusalem after Herod's reconstruction work had finished

By the time of Christ, the Holy Land was an integral part of a prosperous Greco-Roman world. Its connection with desert tents and nomadic life was no more than a romantic memory, like the cowboys and wagon trains of the American West.

With this prosperity came people of real wealth, and they were to be found throughout the Holy Land. They preferred to live near the court in Jerusalem if they were rich and well-placed. But each city had its own wealthy class. There were merchants; there were landowners; and there were craftsmen throughout the land just as in Jerusalem.

"The poor we have with us"

There were the poor as well. When Jesus speaks of the poor and the rich he is speaking of a reality that the people would have known well, no matter where they lived. The years during the life of Jesus were peaceful years, and they were years of prosperity for the people who were in a position to exploit the tranquillity in order to become rich. But often the rich acquired their wealth with no concern for the poor. And that is why we hear so much in the Gospels about the rich and the poor.

We know that there was once a well-to-do society in the Holy Land because marble and sandstone are durable materials. These signs of an earlier prosperity survive the ravages of time. We have little by way of the remains of poverty because mud brick does not survive the passage of two thousand years very well. The poor lived in houses made of sun-dried mud brick, plastered inside if the inhabitants could afford that much, and some form of mud-covered stick roof, domed or curved to allow the rain to drain off. There was prosperity in the Holy Land during the life of Christ. But there is no reason to conclude that the majority of people shared in that prosperity.

The Holy Land — Then and Now

Prosperity or poverty in the countryside depended principally on success in raising crops and herds. Today we think of the Holy Land as at least a semidesert. Was it that way in the time of Jesus? Probably not. There were more forests and somewhat more rainfall. But the difference between the climate and rainfall then and today would not account for a substantially different country.

130

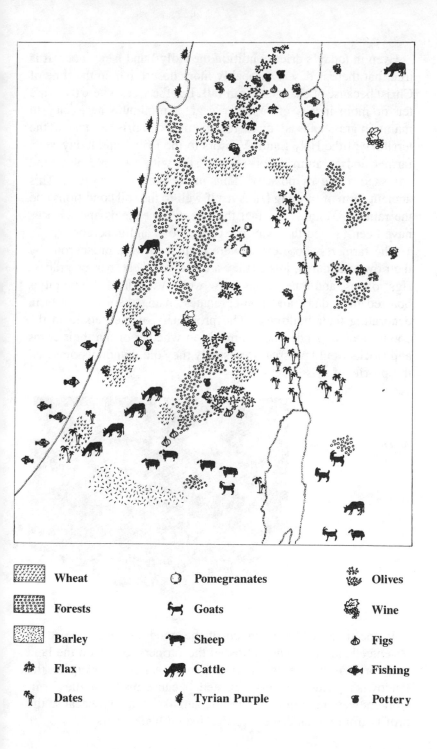

▨	**Wheat**	◐	**Pomegranates**	❧	**Olives**
▦	**Forests**	🐐	**Goats**	🍇	**Wine**
▨	**Barley**	🐑	**Sheep**	♠	**Figs**
❋	**Flax**	🐂	**Cattle**	🐟	**Fishing**
🌴	**Dates**	🌲	**Tyrian Purple**	🏺	**Pottery**

Even in today's drier condition the Holy Land is not poor. It is true that there is desert, probably more desert than in the time of Christ because of changes in rainfall. But the areas where there are ten or more inches of rain per year, a minimum necessary to maintain grasslands adequate for grazing, comprise almost all the territory of the Holy Land. Visitors to the Holy Land today see a farmer and an animal working the soil with a simple plow and envisage a life of poverty. This impression is incorrect. This ancient form of farming lends itself well to the soil conditions and the rainfall. Witness the fact that these same fields and terraces have been farmed this way for generations and generations.

The farmers whose crops were their own were prosperous by their own standards, just as they are today. Wheat, barley, grapes, figs, olives, and other crops grew well in this land. Some cities boasted their dates and pomegranates, using them as motifs in decorating their buildings. The prosperity of the people in the countryside depended not as much on whether or not their crops and flocks would prosper, for usually they did, but on who reaped the profits of the harvest.

An ancient wheat mill

In the time of Christ, much of the good land was owned by absentee landlords. They allowed the farmers to live on the land and care for the herds as long as the real profit went to the landowners. Rural poverty existed because many of the farm-workers were held in an economic serflike state and because the profits from the land went to the distant landowners.

12

BUSINESS AND TRADES
IN THE HOLY LAND

"The kingdom of heaven is like treasure hidden in a field which someone has found; he hides it again, goes off happy, sells everything he owns and buys the field.

Again, the kingdom of heaven is like a merchant looking for fine pearls; when he finds one of great value he goes and sells everything he owns and buys it.

Again, the kingdom of heaven is like a dragnet cast into the sea that brings in a haul of all kinds. When it is full, the fishermen haul it ashore; then, sitting down, they collect the good ones in a basket and throw away those that are no use" (Matthew 13:44-48).

The parables listed above are uncommon. They mention buying and selling. Jesus does not use this kind of parable frequently. His examples are usually less mercantile. Yet, in the Holy Land there were trades and businesses. What were they like? The most documented businesses and trades were those in Jerusalem, so we will begin by describing the business life of Jerusalem. This will give us an initial picture of business life in the country, which we will then expand upon by describing the commerce in the other areas.

Jerusalem was a bustling city, with a large number of inhabitants and an active commercial life. It was not well-situated for trade since it was not on any of the major trading routes. However, its religious and political importance overcame this natural disability and brought commerce to the city. It then became able to support its own local industries.

Skilled Laborers

At the heart of the local industry was the skilled workman working in his own shop. Saint Paul was one of these skilled craftsmen, probably involved in some aspect of making tents. There were spinners and weavers, tanners and leather workers, potters and metalsmiths. There were bakers and water sellers, butchers and oil producers. The production of olive oil, which is mentioned in the Gospels in a few places, was one of the few industries to which the geography lent itself.

These trades were not on a par. Those which produced goods intended for use in the Temple had a higher status. At the bottom were trades like the shipping of goods, which lent themselves to cheating and dishonesty. Dishonesty was not only a civil crime but, to the extent that it violated the integrity of the people, a religious sin. Any trade which placed people in a situation where they could easily break the commandments was looked down on.

The ordinary worship and general repair and maintenance of the Temple required certain trades. Herod's mammoth rebuilding project required even more. Together they brought a period of full employment. There were so many men employed in the reconstruction of the Temple that the completion of the work created a major unemployment crisis in Jerusalem. This crisis was alleviated by hiring the workers to pave the streets of Jerusalem.

The repair and maintenance of the Temple required workers in stone and wood, goldsmiths, mosaic workers, and tile setters.

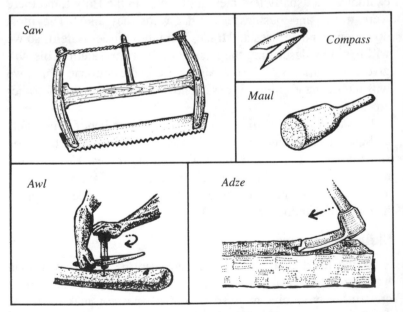

Some carpenters' tools of those days

Money was not spared in embellishing the Temple, so men skilled in luxury trades were numerous. In addition, the hangings in the Temple, which were large and of high quality, had to be renewed periodically, so there was a weaving business specifically oriented to the Temple.

The acts of worship required special trades. Incense was offered daily in the Temple, so there would have been incense makers. Some rites of religious initiation required shaving, so there would have been barbers. Killing unwilling animals is a dangerous occupation. The priests were injured from time to time, so there were doctors.

Unskilled Workers

In addition, there were large numbers of unskilled workers. Most of these workers were poor people. The work they did kept them and their families housed and fed. In other countries in the Greco-Roman world much of the work the poor did was done by slaves. But the Jewish attitude toward slaves, humane for the times, kept them from being the financial asset they were in other parts of the empire, where they could be treated as less than human.

The unskilled workers included some quarry workers, cart drivers, and the men involved in building the aqueducts and sewers. Along with the craftsmen in the building projects, there was a need for large numbers of men to do the work that today is done by machines.

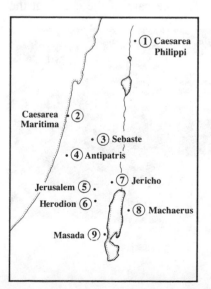

Some of the major building efforts of Herod the Great

1 *Temple to the god Pan*
2 *Harbor and city foundations*
3 *The forum, other public buildings*
4 *Rebuilt ancient town*
5 *Streets widened, the Temple, a palace, other public buildings*
6 *A palace, gardens, a burial place*
7 *A villa named Kypros*
8 *A castle, a villa, a prison*
9 *A summer palace*

135

When we think of the number of fortresses Herod built, such as Kypros, the Herodion, and Masada; the cities he built such as Caesarea Maritima, Antipatris, and Caesarea Philippi; and the Temple, palaces, fortifications, and public utility services he built in Jerusalem, we can understand why his projects were such a boon to the unemployed, unskilled workers throughout the Holy Land.

Jerusalem's function as a pilgrimage center created employment of a seasonal nature. Each year at the festival times, especially at Passover, there was an influx of pilgrims into the Holy City. Providing food, lodging, and sacrificial animals for the pilgrims was another source both of employment and revenue. Estimates of the number of pilgrims vary. However, the population of Jerusalem is set by one scholar at from twenty-five to thirty thousand people. At Passover time, it is estimated that another sixty thousand people came to Jerusalem. These increased numbers taxed supplies of food and water and created an increased sewage and refuse problem. The expanded demands on public services also required more workers.

The Temple was not the only focal point of employment. King Herod and his successors maintained an extensive and well-living court. The rulers also were in the process of embellishing their palaces. In addition to the skilled workers required for the embellishments, there were a number of luxury trades designed to cater to the expensive tastes of the courtiers in dress, cosmetics, and fancy foods. Herod had a number of wives, and each would have her own retinue of relatives and servants. In addition, there were numerous court officials. To take care of the court, at the

Herodion (or Herodium) — the fortress Herod built into the cone of an extinct volcano overlooking Jericho. Although he was buried there, no trace of Herod's remains has been found.

136

level of luxury that had become the standard in Jerusalem, meant employment for many people.

Security Forces

There were, finally, the local security forces. The Temple had its own police force. There were the palace guards. There were the police to handle the pilgrims who came in at Passover and the other festivals. Since large numbers of people always presented the possibility of riots, the security forces had to be adequate to cope with possible trouble. The simple task of locking and unlocking the Temple, palace, and city gates each night and morning required a large number of men.

When we add the security forces, the people involved in the repair and maintenance of the Temple and the normal repairs and sanitation for the city itself, the priests, the men involved in civil administration, the support of the court, those seeing to the upkeep of the palaces, and then add to them the number of men involved in the enormous public works projects begun by King Herod, we can see that the payroll for the city was very large. In many places, people exchanged labor for goods and vice versa. In Jerusalem, it was more common to pay in money. The amount of money changing hands was large.

Public Taxes

How was all this paid for? There were two chief sources, taxation and the Temple treasury. King Herod the Great taxed very heavily, to the point of gaining a reputation for severity. He followed a policy of large governmental expenditures much as we know today. There was a substantial military budget, both to keep order within the kingdom and to protect trade routes from brigandage. He colonized new areas and developed trade resources, all of which were expensive. He maintained a very luxurious and expensive system of palaces, much more expensive than the size of the country would justify. His successors during the life of Christ, both his family members and the Romans in the areas they administered directly, maintained his policies. Needless to say, the tax collectors were kept very busy squeezing out the money to cover these expenses.

The need for tax revenues set the stage for abuses, recorded in all of the New Testament writings. The tax collectors are held up as examples of evildoers. The tax collector, Zacchaeus, mentions to Jesus that "If I have cheated any man then I will pay him back fourfold," an indication that he actually had used his position to extort money. Saint Paul speaks with a provincial administrator who notes that he had to buy Roman citizenship, an indication that money placed in the right hands could assure the granting of privileges. Soldiers are cautioned to "be content with your salary," an indication that they, too, extorted money. Throughout the Gospels the many references to the gap between the rich and the poor, and the sufferings of the poor, point out that the insensitivity of those in power to the poor and powerless was real.

The cost of living in Jerusalem was very high, much higher than in the surrounding area. Because of the number of pilgrims coming into the city and competing for goods and services, because of Herod's numerous public works projects and the high employment rate they brought about, and the continuation of high employment practices by Herod's successors, costs in Jerusalem rose above those of the surrounding country. The projects and the goods and services oriented to the Temple were paid for from the Temple treasury. The treasury, therefore, had to be large and constantly replenished, and it was.

Temple Taxes

Every pious Jew paid an annual tax to the Temple as a sign of his membership in the people. The offering of sacrifices brought in more money. Pilgrims, rich and poor, contributed to the upkeep of the Temple. Rich Jews and some Roman rulers made bequests to the Temple which were so large that they were recorded by historians of the time. But it was the constant flow of pilgrims into the city at the festival times that assured the Temple income. The quantity of gold and silver the Romans looted from the Temple at the time of its capture and burning in A.D. 70, after the great revolt of A.D. 66, was measured in talents. (A talent was a measure of weight, about seventy pounds.) This indicates that the reserves in the Temple were substantial.

What was the economic situation in the rest of the Holy Land? We can give examples that help us grasp the extent of commercial development and how it affected people during the life of Jesus.

The Sea of Galilee or Lake Gennesareth

Other Trades

Peter the apostle was a fisherman, frequently described in later Christian piety as a "simple fisherman." The evidence we find in the Gospel texts, however, and what we know of the fishing industry that Herod developed through subsidies seem to indicate that Peter's work as a fisherman was more commercially developed than often believed.

From the Gospels, we know that Peter was a fisherman, but a fisherman who worked with other fisherman. The Gospels speak of boats and nets, in the plural, and the size of the catch they were capable of handling indicates that Peter and his companions had a small group of fishing boats. Putting this information together with the fact that Peter spoke as the leader of the group allows us to conclude that Peter was the head of a small fishing business.

From other chronicles, we know that Herod fostered the growth of a fishing and fish-processing industry on the Sea of Galilee as part of his plan to develop commerce throughout his kingdom. Money was lent to fishermen for the purchase of nets and boats. Facilities were built on the shore for the drying and salting of fish. However, we would not conclude that the workmen themselves profited from the development. Herod's and his successors' tax collectors squeezed all the profit from the new industries. From the Gospels, we also know that a Gentile, a local centurion, built the synagogue at Capernaum, indicating that the people did not have the means to build it themselves.

Putting this information together, we can conclude not only that Peter was the head of a small fishing business but that the local business did not profit the town. There was a customhouse in town where Saint Matthew had worked, so we can assume that the tax officers were at work in this area as elsewhere, squeezing what they could for themselves and the government now headed by Herod Antipas.

The port city that Herod founded and named after the emperor, Caesarea Maritima, is another good example of the extent of the commercial development and activity during the life of Jesus. The port area itself, which was created artificially, was large and capable of handling many ships. This city is the setting of many important events in the life of the apostles and the early Church.

Part of a stone discovered at Caesarea Maritima. The inscription reads: Pontius Pilate, prefect of Judaea, erected a building in honor of Emperor Tiberius. This is the only nonliterary source we have that refers by name to Pontius Pilate (procurator of Judaea A.D. 25-35).

On the road from Caesarea to Jerusalem is another city rebuilt by Herod and named after his father. Antipatris was a major commercial center. The excavations currently being undertaken show a good-sized city with shops, storage buildings, and small manufacturing areas. The city was at the intersection of the main trade route from Egypt to Mesopotamia and the road from Caesarea on the coast to Jerusalem in the hills. Here, too, the signs indicate an extensive commercial activity. But in this case, some of the profit remained to be used to further embellish a naturally beautiful area. The city is located at the head of the River Yarkon, and is an area of grass and trees which made it a natural resting spot for caravans and travelers.

Herod the Great also built an aqueduct to carry water for irrigation to the fields around his palace in Jericho. Here and in many other places throughout the Holy Land the existence of granaries, storage facilities for wine and olive oil, and the records concerning agricultural villages owned by the royal family indicate that agriculture was extensive.

One of the eight ancient olive trees growing on the traditional site of the Garden of Gethsemane (which means "oil press"). While these trees are certainly not 2,000 years old and the site of Jesus' agony cannot be precisely determined, it must have been at or very near this spot.

We are able, thus, to come up with a picture of a land in which farming, fishing, artisanry, and commerce were developed, more developed than the resources of the land as we see it today would lead us to think. In part, this was due to a climate that was more benign than it is today. But in part, perhaps the greater part, it was due to the determination of the human spirit. The Greek conquerors had determined that they would make this province prosper. The Jews during the days of the Hasmonean rulers had determined that they would make their own land prosperous. Herod the Great left his own ambitious stamp on the Holy Land.

Herod was a Nabataean in part. Nabataea is a monument to the triumph of mind over matter. The Nabataeans established agriculture where normally there should be none; they built cities with a grandeur out of proportion to their geographic importance; they protected but taxed very heavily the caravans that passed through their territory. Herod was one of them and may have applied their ways to his own kingdom.

like Jews today

13
MONEY AND TAXATION

" . . . Master, we know that you are an honest man and teach the way of God in an honest way . . . Tell us your opinion, then. Is it permissible to pay taxes to Caesar or not?'' (Matthew 22:16-17)

" . . . a man whose name was Zacchaeus made his appearance; he was one of the senior tax collectors and a wealthy man . . . Jesus . . . spoke to him: 'Zacchaeus, come down. Hurry, because I must stay at your house today.' And he hurried down and welcomed him joyfully. They all complained when they saw what was happening. 'He has gone to stay at a sinner's house' they said. But Zacchaeus stood his ground and said to the Lord, 'Look, sir, I am going to give half my property to the poor, and if I have cheated anybody I will pay him back four times the amount . . .' '' (Luke 19:1-2,5-9).

In addition to its political and military efforts, the Roman Empire was also a business enterprise. The government held monopolies on some businesses and worked very closely with businessmen in others. From the conquered provinces, the Romans extracted money and basic foods like wheat and olive oil for export back to Rome. Part of this exploitation was the desire to make the provinces profitable to Rome. And part was a real need to cope with the large welfare problem in the city of Rome. The Roman aristocrats despised and feared Rome's urban poor, thousands and thousands of them. They were afraid of the potential power of the slum dwellers should they rise in revolt. Keeping this rabble content required the fear of the law on the one hand, and on the other the peculiar brand of welfare we have come to know as "bread and circuses."

Roman System of Taxation

A significant part of Rome's food and money came from the conquered provinces. It was gathered by a system of taxation more similar to the criminal protection racket of some American cities than to the internal revenue taxation that we know. The tax collectors extorted money from the provinces under threat of severe penalties for nonpayment.

Roman governors frequently bought their offices. Often they mortgaged their family wealth to buy the appointment from the emperor. The governor, in turn, appointed a censor who ran the

Silver coins used in Jesus' lifetime
(Any of these could be the "thirty pieces of silver" of Matthew 26:14.)

(a) Tyre's two-drachma piece. The head of the Tyrian god Melkart (by this time renamed Hercules); (b) imperial denarius of Augustus, minted at Antioch; (c) imperial denarius of Tiberius. The inscription reads: "Tiberius Caesar, august son of the deified Augustus."

Coins of Herod the Great and his sons

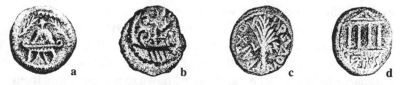

(a) Coin of Herod the Great — crested helmet between two palm branches; (b) coin of Archelaus — a war galley with oars and a battering ram; (c) coin of Antipas — palm branch; (d) coin of Philip — temple at Caesarea Philippi.

Coins of Roman procurators
(Any of these could be the widow's mite of Mark 12:42.)

(a) Coin of Marcus Ambibulus (A.D. 6-9) — palm tree; (b) coin of Valerius Gratus (A.D. 15-26) — vine leaf; (c) coin of Pontius Pilate (A.D. 26-36) — soothsayer's wand.

143

province's tax-collecting office. This office was responsible for raising the funds required to govern the province as well as paying the taxes due to Rome. From the provincial tax revenues, the governor also recovered his own investment in obtaining the office. This could take several years. The governor's hope was to retain the post long enough not only to regain the purchase price but to make a substantial profit as well.

In the Holy Land, the Romans did not collect the local taxes themselves. They used agents, usually local Jews. The censor auctioned off the actual collection of the taxes for five year periods to these local tax collectors, called publicans. The publicans, in effect, were given a franchise to collect taxes. This system had several advantages. First, the locals knew better who had taxable money. This allowed them to raise more in taxes. Also, the anger customarily directed against the tax collectors was directed to the publicans rather than the Roman government. Because anger toward the Romans could lead to an insurrection, it was helpful to have it directed toward someone else.

The tax collectors were allowed to keep the profit from the taxes they raised. The profit was the amount above and beyond the sum they agreed to raise in taxes at the time they bought the office. The Romans chose the agents who could bring in the most money without causing uprisings. It was to the publicans' advantage to be zealous in the service of their Roman masters. But some were known to collect more than they had a right to, as the comment of Zacchaeus indicates. They also were known to accept bribes from the rich, allowing them to pay less than was their due.

Taxes were paid on the production of goods and on the sale of goods. The people found the taxes analogous to our sales taxes expecially burdensome. Taxes or frontier duties were paid by people passing with their goods from one kingdom to another. Judaea and Samaria, on the one hand, and Galilee and Perea, on the other, were separate territories. To go from one to the other required going through customs, as we do today, and required changing currency. Saint Matthew was a frontier customs officer.

The Gospel mentions two taxes, the head tax paid to the Roman authority by each adult and the half-shekel paid to the Temple authority annually by each adult man. Note that the one in charge of the tax-collecting office was called a censor, indicating that the census was taken primarily for tax purposes. In Saint Luke, we read that Joseph went with Mary, his betrothed, to Bethlehem to register because he was of the house and line of David. The registration was part of a census for tax purposes.

We also read of the money changers in the Temple. They were there to change foreign coin, the money brought by the Jewish pilgrims from outside Judaea, into local money. Each person was expected to pay the Temple tax of the half-shekel, and the wealthier were expected to make a donation to the Temple as well. But, as noted previously, foreign money could not be used because it had the graven image of a foreign ruler on it, and graven images were forbidden by the Law.

Roman taxation was galling to the Jews because it touched a sensitive religious nerve. The people believed that their relationship with God was a pact or treaty. To have foreigners ruling their country and to have their country divided, so that a Jew could not pass from one part to another without being taxed, was humiliating. To have Jews collaborating with pagan conquerors in extorting money from other Jews was more than an economic burden or a political offense. To many of the faithful, it said that God had abandoned them. The abandonment was seen as punishment for their sins. This sinfulness called for a religious renewal, a renewal that would include Jewish mastery of Jewish lands and life.

Call for a Free, Autonomous Government

It is in this context of a desire for the establishment of a native, autonomous, and Jewish government that the events of the Gospel are carried out. This hoped for Jewish government would have both religious and political significance and would reestablish the proper order between God and his people. At the different times when the people came to make Jesus king, this is what they had in mind — freedom from this foreign, humiliating, and irreligious control and the establishment of a free and religiously reverent state.

14
ROADS AND ROBBERS

"Jesus was going up to Jerusalem, and on the way he took the Twelve to one side and said to them, 'Now we are going up to Jerusalem . . . ' " (Matthew 20:17-18).

"Jesus said: 'I am the Way . . . ' " (John 14:6).

"Jesus replied, 'A man was once on his way down from Jerusalem to Jericho and fell into the hands of brigands . . . ' " (Luke 10:30).

During the life of Christ, people traveled extensively in the Holy Land. Where were they going, and how did they get there? Most of the people were going to Jerusalem or returning from their religious or commercial trips to Jerusalem. They made use of an unusually extensive system of roads and, for the most part, they walked.

Holy Land Roads

The road system throughout Judaea and some of the nearby provinces was well-developed. Today we think of the Romans as road builders, and indeed they were. But if we think that the Romans came into a land with an underdeveloped road system and installed a good one where none had been, then we would be making a mistake.

Historians point out that there were two major periods of road building in the Holy Land. The first took place in the early days of the kingdom. King Omri and his son King Ahab, who lived several generations after David and Solomon, are examples of the kings who developed the first roads. They were men like Herod the Great. They get very bad coverage in the Old Testament because they were religious renegades. They preferred the green hills of Samaria and trade with the Phoenicians to the more austere life of Jerusalem. Samaria, which Omri founded in 876 B.C., is closer to the coast, closer to the Mediterranean world, and closer to the pagan religions of that world than is Jerusalem, which is fifty miles

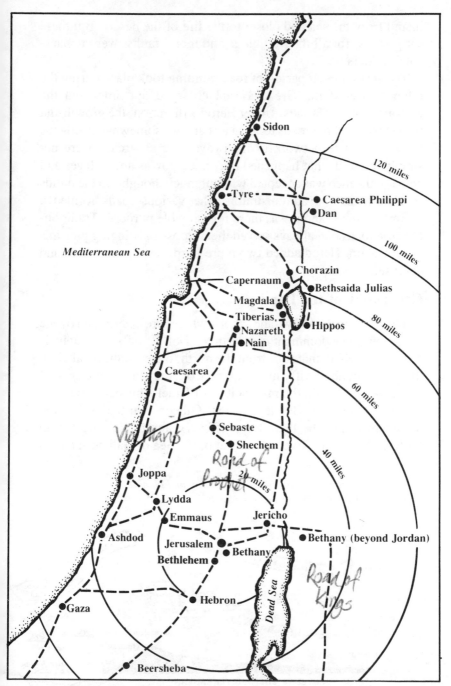

Principal roads of the Holy Land during New Testament times

inland from the sea and closer to the life of the desert. But these early kings, for all their religious and moral faults, were remarkable builders.

The second great period of road building took place during the reign of Herod the Great. Herod enlarged and improved the existing system of roads. Under Herod's direction, the growth and management of the roads took on a character somewhat analogous to our interstate network of highways. Herod's roads were not simply the trails that happened to connect towns and villages and whose existence was accepted without much thought. In the minds of Herod and his administrators, the various roads formed a definite system, and it was there for a double purpose. Traditionally, the roads had always served the purpose of bringing pilgrims to Jerusalem. Herod added two more purposes — commerce and defense.

Geography of the Land

The roads in the Holy Land, as elsewhere, are determined by the geography. The dominant feature in the Holy Land's geography is a mountain chain that runs from the north to the south, paralleling the seacoast, about fifty miles inland from the sea. On the crest of this chain were built the major cities of Israel's history, cities like Hebron, Jerusalem, Bethlehem, and Gibeon. On the east of the mountain chain, the land drops off very abruptly to the Jordan Valley. The Jordan River comes out of the Sea of Galilee and runs

Palestine — section west to east — topography and climate
(Heights are slightly exaggerated for clarity.)

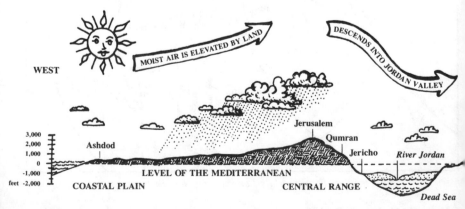

south to the Dead Sea. The farther south the river flows the more forbidding and more desertlike the landscape becomes. The Dead Sea is twelve hundred feet below sea level and the lowest place on earth.

On the other side of the mountain chain, to the west, are rolling hills. These hills are pleasant farm lands, known as the Shephela. And west of these lowland hills is the coastal plain. The coastal plain was agriculturally good land but subject to occasional outbreaks of malaria because of its swamps. Militarily, it was also open to invasion from the sea.

The roads, like the life of the people, were connected to the central mountain chain, known as the hill country of Ephraim and the hill country of Judaea. The roads fell into two basic groups. There were the roads that connected the cities on the crest of the hills, and there were the roads that climbed from the lowlands up the slopes to the crest. The north-south roads, along the crest, were the easier roads to travel. The roads that ran east-west from the lowlands up the crest were obviously more difficult. From Jericho to Jerusalem, for example, is only scarcely twenty miles, but it involves a climb of about three thousand feet.

During the time of Christ, these roads were in good repair. They had to be. With thousands and thousands of pilgrims coming to Jerusalem and with the source of food and building materials several hundred to several thousand feet lower than Jerusalem, the task of bringing supplies to the city was very difficult. Good roads made that task somewhat less difficult.

Block diagram of the Holy Land

149

Kinds of Roads

What were the roads like? To begin with, they were not paved. Road paving did not begin until after the insurrection and repression of A.D. 66-70. They varied from simple trails, wide enough for one person, to roads designed for heavy carts. The main roads were known as the king's highway, which meant that they were kept up by the government. The main roads were marked with curbstones placed along the sides. Rocks jutting into the path were removed. On the steeper slopes, where beasts of burden could slip, steps were cut into the stone. Where necessary, there were terraces to permit passage around steep slopes or through ravines, which were numerous. Most of the east-west roads followed the valleys and gulleys carved out over the centuries by rains. Today, these highways would look like improved trails, and we might hesitate to drive an automobile over one for fear of damaging the tires or the suspension. But for the pedestrians of those days, for farmers with their donkeys, for merchants with their carts loaded with merchandise, and for soldiers with their weapons these roads provided relatively direct access to Jerusalem, to the forts surrounding and protecting Jerusalem, and to the towns and villages in the countryside.

This gives some idea of the main roads. What were the smaller ones like? The key feature in the secondary roads was stones. Each year, as the local farmers plowed the fields, they would turn up more and more stones. Small stones, the size of a fist, could be left lying in the soil, but the larger ones were carried to the sides of the

An ancient stepped street by the side of the Church of St. Peter in Gallicantu. Jesus and his disciples most likely walked on these very steps.

fields where they were placed one on another until they formed walls bordering the fields. Because good soil is scarce in the Holy Land, the roads did not cut across the arable soil but wound around the small plots and passed between the walls on the edges of the fields. The roadways could vary from a width permitting two laden donkeys to pass each other to a small trail wide enough only for a man. The roadway itself varied from stones to exposed bedrock to dry dust, which turned to mud in the rains.

Jesus spoke to his followers using these roads as an example of what it meant to follow him. He said "I am the Way," and by this statement drew their attention to the foot-bruising and wearying experience they all knew so well, travel on the roads of the Holy Land.

A rock-free "main road"

A smaller one-man trail

The Bandits

{ Only way, too!

Travel by road was common and possible. How safe was it? Put simply, it was unsafe. The country was full of brigands or bandits. But this banditry tells us much about the life of the Holy Land because it was the result of many of the situations we have already described. In a word, the banditry was the result of the oppression of the peasants by the rich.

What do we know about the brigands? To begin with, there were a lot of them. They appear to have been peasants driven from their lands by the oppressive taxes of the Romans and the Jewish aristocracy. There are indications that they were more than just common thieves, for they had the sympathy and, in some cases, the protection and collaboration of the peasants. We have come to call such bandits Robin Hoods. They were on the side of the peasants in the class warfare that had developed in the Holy Land.

After the death of Christ, in the year A.D. 66, there was a major uprising against the Romans and their Jewish collaborators. Although this uprising took place about thirty years after the death and Resurrection of Jesus, the situation that brought it about was already developing during the years of his public ministry. What we have referred to as class warfare he spoke about over and over in describing the luxurious life of the rich and the suffering of the poor.

The Romans and Greeks owned many large farms and plantations in the Holy Land. Also, the Jewish aristocrats and the leading priestly families owned large plots of land and, in some cases, entire villages. Their standard of living was very high, as we have already noted. To support that standard of living they squeezed every cent from their lands and from the peasants who farmed those lands.

A productive farm can support more people than it takes to farm it if the produce from that land can be used to support the farmers. In the Holy Land, however, the lion's share of the produce and the profit went to the landowners. As a result, more and more people were driven off the land. Some went to the cities, where they became the beasts of burden who built the palaces, monuments, and fortifications we have described above. Others became bandits. They lived on the edge of the civilized areas, at the places

The Wadi Qilt, which runs from the slopes east of Jerusalem to Jericho. The robbers who preyed upon the travelers of these roads took shelter in this wadi or similar wilderness areas.

where the cultivated lands became wilderness, like the country alongside the road from Jerusalem to Jericho mentioned by Jesus in the parable of the Good Samaritan. From these areas on the edge of the wilderness, they preyed on the trade routes and then fled to their hideouts in the wildernesses.

Banditry was common when Herod the Great became king, but he reduced it by extraordinary effort. Strategically located fortresses, well-disciplined police, a system which rewarded informers, and publicized executions made the roads safer for travel. And his full-employment policies took the edge off the problem of the numbers of landless peasants.

With the death of Herod, around the time that Jesus was born, the problem of banditry again increased. The Roman procurators in Judaea did not maintain a constant policy toward the bandits. Pontius Pilate, for example, was very stern and repressive, executing brigands frequently, while others went to the point of allowing the relatives of the bandits to ransom them from prison.

But the conditions that drove the peasants off the land continued. The sympathy of the peasants for the bandits continued. And the bandits continued to prey on the rich, on their country estates and on the trade routes. As a result, travel by road involved some element of risk.

153

CONCLUSION

For three years Jesus walked these roads of Palestine. In the summer's fierce, semidesert heat and in the cold wind and rain of winter he walked up and down this rugged land. His way led him through clothes-penetrating limestone dust, across plates of polished bedrock exposed by eroding years, and along paths of ankle-twisting stones. In the end, he was put to death between two of the brigands whose forays from out of the cliffs and wadis made travel unsafe. And, ironically, his preaching and ministry were directed often enough to these very same landless poor. He took on their lot, and eventually suffered the worst it had to offer.

The events of Jesus' life — his birth, ministry, death, and Resurrection — all took place in a well-defined setting. We know about his land, its history and its culture. The history, the politics, the economics, and the religion of Christ's Palestine are woven through the events of his life, the subject of his teaching, the examples he used, and the way he ministered. In being the Christ for people of all times, he was also a man with a history conditioned by the realities of his own time. So his life and his teachings, as recorded in the Gospels, are expressed within the context of the events that shaped Palestine and the Near East during the early days of the Roman Empire.

The Gospels, like the Church itself, come out of this land and out of this time. To understand the Gospels it helps to understand the land and the time. Because the Gospels are often the answers to questions, they can help us to know what the questions are. Because the answers are stated using the words and the examples and the experiences of first-century Palestinian life, we can better understand the issues raised in the Gospels and the very ways they are raised if we understand what it was like to live in the Holy Land during the time of Jesus.

That has been the purpose of this book — to look at the background of the Gospels so we could understand them better. First, we looked at the political background. The rulers mentioned in the Gospels at the birth of Jesus, and again at his death, controlled their peoples and their territories with an iron hand.

Understanding the strength, even the cruelty, of that grip can help us see how the promise of freedom would have appealed to people living under such oppression. To this end, Jesus quoted Isaiah when he preached at Nazareth for the first time:

> The spirit of the Lord Yahweh has been given to me,
> for Yahweh has anointed me.
> He has sent me to bring good news to the poor,
> to bind up hearts that are broken;
> to proclaim liberty to captives,
> freedom to those in prison;
> to proclaim a year of favour from Yahweh,
> a day of vengeance for our God (Isaiah 61:1-2).

Today the Church and the followers of Christ still try to make these words, which were addressed originally to a small group of people in a particular setting, applicable to all people.

The cultural background is equally important. No influence was felt as strongly in the Jewish culture of Palestine as the influence of the Greeks. Administratively, militarily, economically, and culturally the Greeks had put their stamp on the land of Christ. They also attempted to change the religion of the Jewish people, and the religious struggles in which Jesus found himself reflected this tug-of-war between those supporting and those opposed to Greek influence. It is interesting to note, however, that Jesus usually sidestepped these controversies, focusing his attention on the religious education of the people and criticizing the religious leaders who used their public roles for their own private purposes.

Again, in the Church today, the effort we make to reform our lives is principally an attempt to make the Church's treasures, both spiritual and physical, more readily accessible to the people who need them. We try to be motivated by the same sense of compassion that was so evident in the life and ministry of Christ.

Few aspects of Jewish life in Palestine touch on the Gospels as strongly as do the dictates of the Jewish religion. That Jesus should be referred to as the "Lamb of God who takes away the sins of the world" makes little sense, other than as a poetic image, unless we understand the role of the lamb in Jewish sacrifice. And that Jesus' geneology should be traced showing his descent from King David again has little importance unless we grasp the role of descent in

Jewish religion, especially in Jewish hopes for a Messiah. For these reasons, we looked into the basics of Jewish religion in Palestine during Jesus' time.

Money and social class also enter into the Gospels. Jesus preached principally to the poor and the powerless, moved by their plight. What was their situation? Who had the money in Palestine, and how was it used? The moral teachings of Jesus make more sense if we understand the quality of morals in his time. Important in this understanding is the role that greed and insensitivity to the poor played in Palestinian culture.

We study the cultural, economic, and religious background of those times principally so that we may better understand the inspired words of the Gospels. These sacred writings are a treasure valued by Christians in all places and of all times, but they were written for specific people in a specific place at a specific time. Their influence and their purpose transcend their historical context, but they are written very much within the context of Jesus' world. So that we may bring the message of Jesus into our twentieth century we have to enter into that first-century world as best we can. By trying to do this in our minds and hearts, we are able to get the feel of what it must have been like to live in the Holy Land at the time of Christ.

The introductory chapter proposed an analogy that the author thought the reader would find useful in studying the political, cultural, religious, and economic background of Jesus' life. The reader's attention was directed toward the most sacred place in the Christian world, the quarry that King Herod's men had excavated just outside the walls of Jerusalem. This site was "of special interest to us . . . not only because it is the holiest place in the Holy Land but also because it sums up the difficulties we face in trying to reconstruct history." At the conclusion of this book this same most sacred place is pointed to again. This time, however, it's meant to serve not merely as a study aid but, more importantly, as a flashpoint enkindling our faith in the saving events which took place there.

And at the ninth hour Jesus cried out in a loud voice, "Eloi, Eloi, lama sabachthani?" which means, *"My God, my God, why have you deserted me?"* When some of those who stood by heard this, they said, "Listen, he is calling on Elijah." Someone ran and soaked a sponge in vinegar and, putting it on a reed, gave it him to drink saying, "Wait and see if Elijah will come to take him down." But Jesus gave a loud cry and breathed his last. And the veil of the Temple was torn in two from top to bottom. The centurion, who was standing in front of him, had seen how he had died, and he said, "In truth this man was a son of God."

It was now evening, and since it was Preparation Day . . . there came Joseph of Arimathaea . . . and he boldly went to Pilate and asked for the body of Jesus. Pilate, astonished that he should have died so soon, summoned the centurion and enquired if he was already dead. Having been assured of this by the centurion, he granted the corpse to Joseph who bought a shroud, took Jesus down from the cross, wrapped him in the shroud and laid him in a tomb which had been hewn out of the rock. He then rolled a stone against the entrance to the tomb.

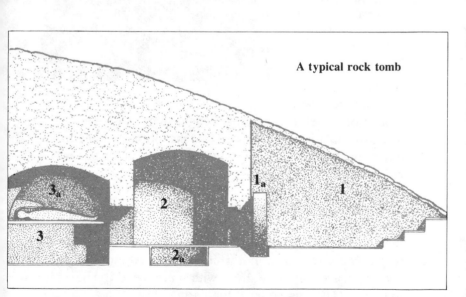

A typical rock tomb

(1) Open passage with steps; (1$_a$) large rolling stone; (2) room, with benches against the walls (2$_a$); (3) burial room, with wall niches in which the dead were placed (3$_a$). After a time only the skeleton remained. These bones were collected and placed in a small chest called an ossuarium.

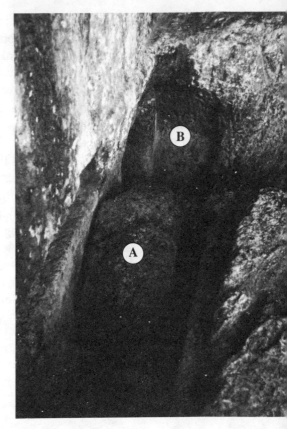

The entry to the tomb complex of Queen Helena of Adiabene. It provides a typical example of the many rock tombs found in the Holy Land. A large wheel-like stone (A) — sometimes weighing as much as a ton — was set into a carved groove (B). After the burial, the stone could be rolled down the inclined track to seal the tomb.

When the sabbath was over, Mary of Magdala, Mary the mother of James, and Salome, bought spices with which to go and anoint him. And very early in the morning on the first day of the week they went to the tomb, just as the sun was rising.

They had been saying to one another, "Who will roll away the stone for us from the entrance to the tomb?" But when they looked they could see that the stone — which was very big — had already been rolled back. On entering the tomb they saw a young man in a white robe seated on the right-hand side, and they were struck with amazement. But he said to them, "There is no need for alarm. You are looking for Jesus of Nazareth, who was crucified: he has risen, he is not here. See, here is the place where they laid him" (Mark 15:34-39,42-46, 16:1-6).

nice little work, really

add to bibliography

FOR FURTHER READING

The Encyclopaedia Britannica (Chicago) and the *New Catholic Encyclopedia* (McGraw-Hill, New York) are available in most libraries and contain historical, geographical, archaeological, and biblical articles.

The Jerome Biblical Commentary (Prentice-Hall, Inc., Englewood Cliffs, New Jersey) and John McKenzie's *Dictionary of the Bible* (Macmillan, New York) are also commonly available and can explain single texts and single topics.

Hengel, Martin. *Judaism and Hellenism: Studies in Their Encounter in Palestine During the Early Hellenistic Period,* trans. John Bowden. Philadelphia: Fortress Press, 1981. Describes the encounter between the two cultures in considerable depth.

Jeremias, Joachim. *Jerusalem in the Time of Jesus: An Investigation into Economic & Social Conditions During the New Testament Period,* trans. F. H. Cave & C. H. Cave. Philadelphia: Fortress Press, 1975.

Reicke, Bo I. *The New Testament Era.* Philadelphia: Fortress Press. Describes the Holy Land from 500 B.C. until A.D. 100.

Wilkinson, John. *Jerusalem As Jesus Knew It: Archaeology As Evidence.* London: Thames Hudson, Ltd., 1978. A lucid and scholarly guide to the sites in and around Jerusalem that can be legitimately linked to Jesus.

Yamauchi, Edwin. *Harper's World of the New Testament.* San Francisco: Harper & Row, 1981. An informative description of the first century and the cultural context of early Christianity.

OTHER HELPFUL BOOKS FROM LIGUORI

DISCOVERING THE BIBLE
Book One and Book Two
by Reverend John Tickle
Focusing on 8 key themes in the Scriptures, each book moves from the Old to the New Testament with sessions featuring Background, Scripture References, Discussion Questions, and Concluding Prayer Service. Book One includes themes on Revelation, Covenant, Redemption, Messiah, etc. Book Two continues the program and includes themes on Hospitality, Worship, Justice, Discipleship, etc. $3.95 each

JESUS' PATTERN FOR A HAPPY LIFE: THE BEATITUDES
by Marilyn Norquist
A beautiful, joy-filled book which invites you to consider the Beatitudes as a pattern for peace — a plan that CAN be followed in today's world. In the Sermon on the Mount, Jesus gave us a pattern for daily life in his Kingdom, a way to face troubles and problems and still find peace, hope, and joy. $2.95

Handbook of the Bible Series, $1.50 each
by Marilyn Norquist
HOW TO READ AND PRAY THE GOSPELS
This book was written to help the average person read and understand the Bible. It offers prayer suggestions, ideas for family use, questions for discussion to help get into the Scriptures and learn to really enjoy the Bible.

HOW TO READ AND PRAY SAINT PAUL
Brings the letters of Saint Paul to life — as actual letters which were written to real people who were searching for answers, just as we are today.

HOW TO READ AND PRAY THE PROPHETS
This book will give new meaning to the familiar Sunday Scripture readings from the Old Testament prophets. It delves into the beauty of their writings and the deep spirituality they offer for the people of today. For people who are seeking justice and deeper relationships with others and God — just as the prophets did.

Order from your local bookstore or write to:
Liguori Publications, Box 060, Liguori, Missouri 63057
(Please add 50¢ for postage and handling.)